1989
THE GREAT GRAND FINAL

TONY WILSON

Produced in 2020 by The Slattery Media Group

First published in 2020 by Hardie Grant Books, an imprint of Hardie Grant Publishing

Hardie Grant Books (Melbourne)
Wurundjeri Country
Building 1, 658 Church Street
Richmond, Victoria 3121

Hardie Grant Books (London)
5th & 6th Floors
52–54 Southwark Street
London SE1 1UN

hardiegrantbooks.com

Hardie Grant acknowledges the Traditional Owners of the country on which we work, the Wurundjeri people of the Kulin nation and the Gadigal people of the Eora nation, and recognises their continuing connection to the land, waters and culture. We pay our respects to their Elders past, present and emerging.

All rights reserved. No part of this publication may be reproduced, stored in a retrieval system or transmitted in any form by any means, electronic, mechanical, photocopying, recording or otherwise, without the prior written permission of the publishers and copyright holders.

The moral rights of the author have been asserted.

Copyright text © Tony Wilson 2020
Copyright photography © AFL Photos 2020, Newspix 2020
Unless otherwise marked, photos by AFL Photos. These photos can be purchased at aflphotos.com.au
Cover images © Wayne Ludbey

®™ The AFL logo and competing team logos, emblems and names used are all trademarks of and used under licence from the owner, the Australian Football League, by whom all copyright and other rights of reproduction are reserved. Australian Football League, AFL House, 140 Harbour Esplanade, Docklands, Victoria, Australia, 3008.

 A catalogue record for this book is available from the National Library of Australia

1989 The Great Grand Final

ISBN 9781743796566

10 9 8 7 6 5 4 3

Publisher: Geoff Slattery
Editors: Geoff Slattery and Russell Jackson
Designer: Kate Slattery

Printed in Australia by Griffin Press, an Accredited ISO AS/NZS 14001 Environmental Management System printer.

 The paper this book is printed on is certified against the Forest Stewardship Council® Standards. Griffin Press – a member of the Opus Group holds chain of custody certification SCS-COC-001185. FSC® promotes environmentally responsible, socially beneficial and economically viable management of the world's forests.

COVER: Geelong's Steve Hocking (left) and Hawthorn's Dermott Brereton exchange pleasantries early in the 1989 Grand Final. Brereton's teammate, Jason Dunstall, and umpire Peter Cameron (right) attempt to restore order. Wayne Ludbey photo. Used with permission.

BACK COVER: Coach Allan Jeans shows off the spoils of victory, as he is carried from the field by Peter Curran (left) and John Kennedy (right), with captain Michael Tuck and teenager Greg Madigan on Kennedy's right. Wayne Ludbey photo. Used with permission.

1989
THE GREAT GRAND FINAL

TONY WILSON

Hardie Grant
BOOKS

CONTENTS

Introduction 7

1. Seeing the Light 11
2. Humps and Bumps 16
3. Using Initiative 20
4. A Matter of Trust 23
5. Extra volatility 28
6. From why to How 34
7. A new diet 39
8. Running out of time 42
9. The Bridge 48
10. Wonder Coach 51
11. You'll keep 54
12. Not Far Away 57
13. Torrential 62
14. Angry Young Men 65
15. Demolition Dermott 69
16. Tribunal Night 73
17. Where's Langers? 77
18. Up All Night 81
19. The Biggest Job 84
20. A Brownlow Premonition 88
21. Selection Night 91
22. The Plan 97
23. The Competitive Beast ... 99
24. The pointed gun 103
25. An Awkward Truth 109
26. Floating 112
27. Four seconds 115
28. You Champion 120
29. The Tripod 122
30. The fights go on 124
31. The Understudy 127
32. Spinning Eyes 131
33. "It's yours, Dipper" 134
34. I'm still here 138
35. Memory loss 141

1989
THE GREAT GRAND FINAL

36	Still attacking	145	55	Pain and Exhaustion ... 213
37	Pure athletic poetry	148	56	Not far away ... 216
38	Two silverbacks	154	57	The reason ... 219
39	The pendulum	158	58	More reasons ... 224
40	Blood and bubble wrap	161	59	High art ... 228
41	Pay the Price	165	60	A Beautiful Anachronism ... 232
42	Bang	170	61	Just one Saturday in September ... 235
43	Running off	174	62	Idiosyncrasies ... 238
44	Emergency lights	177	63	The Secret Lair ... 241
45	The Scallywag	181	64	Postscript ... 245
46	Broken bodies	184			
47	The Achilles Heel	187			
48	It's all happening	189			
49	Other courage	193			
50	The Miracle Man	195			
51	Fine piece of machinery	198			
52	Number Nine	201			
53	The Siren	205			
54	The thing about Dipper	210			

Acknowledgements ... 248

The 1989 Finals Of Hawthorn and Geelong ... 250

1989 Grand Final game stats ... 251

1989 Grand final line-up ... 252

Bibliography ... 253

For my father, Ray Wilson.
And, in memory of Michael Gordon,
the great keeper of Hawthorn stories.

INTRODUCTION

I played zero games for Hawthorn between 1989 and 1992. I know that description covers most of us, but I was a listed player during that time, first with the under-19s (1989-91) and then the seniors (1992), so they had to *actively* not select me—which they managed to do.

It was nevertheless a thrilling time of my life, if ultimately heartbreaking. The senior team dazzled on and off the field, and even to be on the periphery filled my late teenage years with hope and pride. In 1989 the under-19s trained on the seniors' off nights, Mondays and Wednesdays, but my heroes were constantly *there* at Glenferrie Oval—lifting weights, receiving medical treatment, practising their goal-kicking, thumping balls at each other in the nets, laughing, joking, boxing, jogging out the weekend's aches and pains.

One Wednesday night I walked up the race and almost bumped into the huge, ripped torso of the most famous Hawthorn player of the era. He stuck out his hand: "G'day, Dermott Brereton." I was 16 years old and barely used to adult handshakes. "Tony Wilson," I squeaked. "Are you with the under-19s out there?" Dermott asked. I nodded that I was. "Well, welcome to the club. We're all one club here. If you ever want to have a chat about your footy, come and say hello."

It was like meeting a muscle-bound, peroxided, permed, stud-ear ringed Don Corleone. Three years later I'd experience the wonder of signing autographs for a group of young female fans while leaning against Dermott's red Ferrari. "This is Willo. You'll want Willo's autograph too one day," he told them.

No, they wouldn't. I was placed on the senior list in November of 1991 as a father-son selection—my dad, Ray Wilson, played for the Hawks between 1966 and 72 including the 1971 premiership—and then removed from it before the June draft of the following year. My single 'goal-setting' meeting with Hawthorn coach Alan Joyce was prophetic and short. Said Joyce, with his typical knack for warmth and pleasantries: "We think your shins are a problem and so we'll modify your program. If you get stress fractures again, we'll get rid of you." They barely modified my program. I got stress fractures again. They got rid of me. A year or so later, the AFLPA fought for a collective bargaining agreement that guaranteed rookies the security of two-year minimum contracts and base salaries. The shortness and shittiness of my AFL non-career may never be matched.

But in 1989 those disappointments were still in the future.

In 1989 Dermott, Dunstall, Dipper, Platten and the other stars I've interviewed for this book were at the centre of the Hawthorn firmament, and I was giddily happy in my outer orbit, playing in the under-19s under their premiership teammate Russell Greene. All of this is to say that this isn't quite an *insider* account of what is widely considered to be the greatest Grand Final ever played, but nor am I a typical sportswriter when it comes to analysing the Hawthorn players of this era. I loved them then—they were the heroes I grew up barracking for and the footballers I wanted to be. In a glorious era for the club, I was thereabouts, without being *there*.

I was also in the Olympic Stand of the MCG on 30 September 1989, when these heroes played another set of heroes from Geelong in a Grand Final that was recognised immediately as an all-time classic. As the years have unfolded and the game of footy has evolved,

INTRODUCTION

that status has, if anything, been enhanced. It had a tight finish but was incredibly high scoring. There were one-on-one contests all over the ground between players who were stars of the game, personality players, many of whom became legends. There was one individual performance so breathtakingly graceful that to watch it was as much about understanding artistry as sport. And the game was tough, bordering on dangerously violent—and that's good for the story, even if it's not good for football.

So here it is, my favourite game of footy ever played.

1989. The Great Grand Final.

—Tony Wilson, January 2020

1

SEEING THE LIGHT

There are 12 seconds left in the 1989 Grand Final when Hawthorn's Robert DiPierdomenico becomes the last person to touch the ball in the VFL era.

The ball is bounced in the centre of the MCG. Hawthorn leads a fast-finishing Geelong by six points. Cats ruckman Darren Flanigan palms it to on-baller Andrew Bews, who shapes to kick, a clearance now being the last breath of a chance for the charging Cats. That chance evaporates as DiPierdomenico and his teammate Peter Curran arrive from opposite directions with the force of two armies. A pincer movement in military speak. 'The Malachi Crunch' in the smash-up-derby parlance of *Happy Days*. Simultaneously they tackle Bews, the ball spills, and as the pack collapses to the ground, DiPierdomenico uses his left arm and what remains of his strength to rake the ball out from between the legs of Geelong veteran Neville Bruns. Everywhere there are tired bodies, men barely able to stand. The umpire whistles for another bounce. Then, siren. "Ladies and gentlemen, you've just seen a classic," intones TV commentator Dennis Cometti.

'Dipper' emerges, clutching the footy. He is too exhausted, too wounded, to celebrate in his inimitable style. Every Hawk within kicking distance has both arms raised in jubilation, but not Dipper; his final lunge for the Sherrin is the last time his hands leave his sides. His battering-ram body shrinks under the arm of his captain Michael Tuck, a tentative embrace. Tuck has seven fresh stitches in his hand, blood from the split webbing of two fingers saturating a temporary bandage. "We've won, we've won, we've won," he says to a shrunken Dipper, who hasn't the energy to speak. They have both played seven consecutive Grand Finals in the brown and gold, and this brings their win-loss ledger to 4-3. More importantly, it completes the back-to-back premiership ambition that has burned within this group of players, that has consumed their coach, Allan Jeans.

The Geelong players bow their heads, feeling the crumpling weight of defeat. In the first quarter, they trailed by 42 points. To have come as close as six points is a small miracle, but their faces reveal that only the full miracle would do. They almost delivered it. If the game starts at quarter-time, the Cats win by five goals. Full-forward Gary Ablett has played the most exhilarating individual game in Grand Final history: nine goals one, equalling Collingwood legend Gordon Coventry's Grand Final tally set in 1928. It's not just those goals. Ablett has electrified football's biggest stage with a virtuoso display of speed, acceleration, skill, strength and power. It says something for his genius, and the form he is in, that he was even better the week before; in the preliminary final against Essendon his return was 23 disposals and 8.5. Ablett's four finals have yielded 27 goals and 16 behinds, a mark that surely will never be matched. When he receives the least contentious Norm Smith Medal in the award's history, he gives the shortest of speeches: "I would like to congratulate Hawthorn and thank God for making it all possible."

By then DiPierdomenico, the man whose lung Ablett punctured in the first quarter is on his way to hospital. In the moments after his embrace with Tuck, Dipper collapses to turf. The Hawthorn trainers arrive and escort him from the arena. There's some urgency now. His neck is blowing up like a bullfrog. Whatever adrenaline and willpower had sustained the rambunctious, talismanic 1986 Brownlow medallist until the game's conclusion has deserted him now. *Herald* reporter Shane Templeton is standing next to the race as Dipper hobbles up it, and the sight and sound of what happens next stays with him forever, so that he can recall in awed tones: "I could actually hear the air hissing out of his lungs," Templeton says. "It was frightening, and he was doubled over. The ambulance was parked at the inside door of the rooms and thank heavens it was. The paramedics bundled him into the ambulance and headed off. If they hadn't been there, I hate to think what might have happened. It was a scary end to the game."

DiPierdomenico receives a shot of adrenaline as the ambulance speeds to the nearby St Vincent's Hospital. He is admitted to emergency and lies on a gurney, struggling to breathe. As early as half-time he'd wondered if something was wrong. The skin on his chest and shoulders had dimpled, he says, "like it was turning into bubble wrap." When he pressed the protrusions with his finger, he could hear a soft popping sound. "And my voice was going really high," DiPierdomenico says. "So, I'm running back on the ground after half-time squeaking, "Kick it to me, kick it to me," and I'm thinking, '*what the fuck's going on here?*'

What *was* going on medically was a pneumothorax, or collapsed lung, resulting in subcutaneous emphysema—air leaking from the thoracic cavity into the region under the skin. "I just imploded like the Michelin Man!' is how the perennially colourful Dipper later explains it. Lying on his hospital gurney, air hissing from his lung, still wearing his sweat- soaked Hawthorn jumper. "I felt peaceful," Dipper says. "I really felt peaceful. I felt okay. I wasn't thinking about the game. I wasn't thinking about anything. I'm just lying there, staring into this light, still with my jumper on. Somebody grabs my hand and I thought it was my wife or something, but it was the hospital priest. Just talking softly in my ear."

Dipper is a storyteller, and this is his grandest tale, the one most frequently retold, its narrative pattern a familiar monologue. His teammates now tease him about the light and the priest, and chuckle at Dipper's poetic licence. His former teammate John Kennedy Jnr asks, laughing, "Have you spoken to him yet?". "Did he tell you about the light, how he saw the light when he was nearly dead? And then he wakes up the next morning and notices there's a skylight in the ceiling! Fair dinkum! But it was a courageous effort, nonetheless."

Dipper's life was saved by an emergency intervention. According to his memory, a nurse runs into the room, cuts his premiership guernsey up the centre, and into the famous barrel chest, plunges a needle. "She just goes bang with the needle," Dipper says. "It looked like a knitting needle. It released the air that had been building up under the skin. Without her, I might have been pretty close to moving on."

I ask him whether it was definitely a nurse with the needle. "Doctors and nurses, whatever. But I remember her cutting the jumper. As soon as the needle went in, I began to feel a bit better. A friend of mine reckons she was just with the nurse that did it! She's from Frankston. I'd like to meet up with that nurse and find out what she remembers of it."

Dipper's hospital stay lasts six days. He misses the celebrations, although on the Monday his teammates visit and present him with his medal and the premiership Cup.

Jeans apologises. Unaware of Dipper's situation, at three-quarter time, a full 90 minutes into Dipper's ordeal, Jeans had berated his wingman, sensing a drop in his work rate. "(Neville) Bruns is getting a few kicks, son!" Jeans yelled. "You've got to get on the bike, Robert. You've got to run, and run, and run. I have never seen a boy die of exhaustion out there yet!"

"I fucking nearly did!" Dipper now roars, almost 30 years later. "Nobody's ever died on the field of tiredness. I nearly did!"

Jeans's apology, as Dipper recalls, is coupled with a bedside thank you. "Now listen son," he says, "What you did for the football club and what you've done for your family and what you did for me, I want to thank you from the bottom of my heart."

At Dipper's bedside in those days is his anxious wife, Cheryl. "It's a horrible thing to think about, he's just very, very lucky they got to him in time," she tells *The Sunday Sun's* visiting football writer, Scot Palmer. "I would be quite happy if he said he was going to retire tomorrow." When Dipper is discharged, the club sends him and Cheryl to Queensland's Magnetic Island for two weeks of rest and recuperation.

On Dipper's return, "tanned and wearing a white suit", he must face the Tribunal, a full month after knocking Garry Hocking's teeth out with his forearm during the third quarter of the game that brought him his fifth and final premiership medallion and almost cost him his life. He cops a five-match ban, his fifth and final suspension.

A complicated hero is Dipper.

2

HUMPS AND BUMPS

Malcolm Blight was sitting in his office at SPD Transport in Maribyrnong, eating a sandwich and reading a story in the newspaper about Geelong sacking its coach, John Devine, when the telephone rang. "Hi Malcolm, it's Ken Gannon from the Geelong Football Club," said the man on the line. Blight remembers laughing, "Wow, Ken, I've just been reading about you!"

During the 1988 season Blight's analytical talents had shone in the special-comments role on Channel Seven's footy coverage. He was different from everyone who had come before. He was not only eloquent, passionate, and with the credibility that comes from winning a Brownlow and two premiership medallions, but there was an educational leaning to his commentary that set him apart.

"He's guiding the ball to his foot incorrectly."

"If he runs that way, the ball will go that way."

"His hands are too flat there—when you mark you shape your hands like you're putting a balloon on a mantelpiece."

Blight's charisma radiated from television screens. If the call from

Ken Gannon, Geelong's General Manager, surprised Blight, it didn't surprise the football world.

Despite being just 38 years of age, Blight was already a coach of considerable experience. In 1981 he'd spent 16 games as the VFL's last playing-coach at North Melbourne. His team won six and lost ten. There's a reason why there are no playing coaches today. In round 14 against Richmond, Blight infamously walked into an open goal and dribbled it over the line for a behind, a howler from a champion player with too much on his mind. Blight kicked 4.8 that day, North lost, and he remembers trying to instruct a couple of first-year rookies after the game on kicking technique. "I could see their eyes begin to roll, after all, I'd kicked four goals eight. I'd kicked worse than anyone! The world was changing before my eyes," he says.

After round 16 of 1981 Blight saw the light and handed the job to his 1977 premiership teammate Barry Cable. The next week Blight booted 11.6 against Footscray. The following year he kicked 103 goals, won the Coleman and retired from the VFL, moving home to Adelaide as playing coach for his beloved Woodville. In 1985 he kicked 125 goals for the Warriors, and was made All Australian, 13 years after he first achieved the honour in 1972. In this book there'll be superlatives describing the playing genius of Gary Ablett. Never forget the playing genius of his coach, Malcolm Blight.

Between 1983 and 1987 Blight coached Woodville to its most successful era, an unfortunately low bar to clear; not even the club's favourite son could drag it into a first Grand Final. But he did steer the team to a preliminary final in 1986, chalking up the club's first two finals victories, before falling to eventual premier Glenelg by 21 points. Presented with plenty of chances to win the game, Blight's men booted 2.10 in the last quarter to Glenelg's 3.0. Despite that heartache, Blight rates the 1986 Woodville ride as "equal to any buzz I experienced in footy".

Blight's reputation as a free thinker, a trier of ideas, an innovator, a footy savant, was fostered in those Woodville years. In round 9 of that

1986 season, with his team trailing Port Adelaide badly at Football Park, rather than deliver yet another stinging three-quarter time rebuke, Blight lined his players up in rows and ordered 'lane work'. For another pre-match address, he cut a heart-shaped hole in an opposition jumper and fixed the 'heart' in place with tape. Then as he thundered to his crescendo, he literally *ripped the heart out of the opposition*. "We lost the game," Blight laughs.

In 1987, his final season at Woodville, the team started the year well but faded to fifth. In the elimination final, Glenelg led the Warriors by 63 points at three-quarter time, at which point Blight announced his retirement! To the players. On the ground.

By that time Blight had risen through the ranks to be general manager at SPD Transport, soon to be Brambles Transport, and the balance of work, footy and a young family had proved overwhelming. In the following months, he and his family moved to Melbourne, where he took up the national manager role at SPD. Then Channel Seven called. Then, at the end of the 1988 season, the call came from Geelong's Ken Gannon.

Blight met with and presented before the Geelong Board at Board member Colin Carter's house in Camberwell. He laid out his football philosophies, some borrowed from the football canon passed from Len Smith to Norm Smith, then to Ron Barassi, Blight's coach at North. But a lot of material was pure Malcolm Blight, his thoughts from a lifetime in footy. To accompany his presentation, Blight provided a one-page handout—an outline of how he saw the Cats' game evolving. The essence of what he told the Board can be stated in a simple sentence: *The aim of the game is to score goals quickly.*

"It's not golf," Blight says plainly, but with the charisma that must have lit up that room in Camberwell so many years ago. "It's not *the lowest* score wins. It's the *highest score* wins. So, the aim was always: what can we do better to go out and score goals quickly?"

Helping him score goals quickly was an array of talented forwards who hadn't yet clicked: Ablett, Bill Brownless, Bruce Lindner, Barry

Stoneham and David Cameron. "1989 will be the year for improvement at Geelong," Blight said three days after the 1988 Grand Final, at the press conference that heralded his appointment. "I think the word 'potential' has been used about Geelong, and that's probably right. My job will be to smooth out the humps and bumps."

In 1988 Geelong had won 10 games and finished ninth. In the 1989 home and away season Blight smoothed out the humps and bumps so well that Geelong won 16 games and scored a record-breaking 2916 points at an average of 132.5 points a game, a tally only ever surpassed by Blight's 1992 Cats. Of the 20 highest scores ever kicked, four belong to Blight era Geelong. In the Grand Final, the Cats kicked 21.12 (138), still the 14th highest Grand Final total in League history.

The problem was that Hawthorn kicked 21.18 (144).

3

USING INITIATIVE

Allan Jeans was an attacking coach too.

In terms of persona, he had none of Malcolm Blight's swashbuckling élan. To the media, he spoke quietly and guardedly, his tightly clipped words falling into well-worn grooves of cliché and homily. He praised his players. He respected the opposition. He had wispy hair and elongated ears. He dressed conservatively—pressed pants, V-necked club sweaters and thin-rimmed, grandfatherly glasses.

When he was appointed Hawthorn coach on the 30 September 1980, Jeans had been a full-time police officer since 1958. The law and order occupation played into the public image: respectable, conservative, upstanding, dour. He talked softly and slowly about his desire to turn out players who were 'solid citizens'. He specialised in stony silences that hinted at a temper, but his gentlemanly words and deeds were always beyond reproach. He assumed the public image of a man much older than his years, partly because he'd been the youngest non-playing coach in history when St Kilda appointed him at just

27 years of age for the 1961 season. By 1989 that seemed an age ago. Jeans had been around forever.

When the Hawks first embarked on their search for a coach after sacking David Parkin in 1980, club goalkicking legend Peter Hudson had been the favourite to get the job, but his asking price was too high—$75,000 a year to cover the cost of hiring a locum manager for his Hobart hotel. Reportedly, Jeans had taken the job for less than $20,000 a year.

And yet St Kilda people knew what an extraordinary force Jeans was. In his first year he took the lowly Saints to their first finals series since 1939 and in 1965 to their first Grand Final since 1913. In 1966 he steered the competition's one-time easybeats to their first premiership, still their only flag, the holiest of holies. In the 1971 Grand Final, Jeans's Saints led John Kennedy Snr's Hawks by 20 points at three-quarter time. It was a wet day and a brutal Grand Final. Somehow the Hawks rallied in the last term to win an all-time classic.

My father, Ray Wilson, came on in the second half of that Grand Final for Hawthorn. There's a moment in the third quarter when the 179cm Ray Wilson crashes into Saints enforcer Carl Ditterich and lays him on his backside. Dad's had a T-shirt made from the grainy TV image. He says as that clash has been mentioned to him a thousand times since, he might as well be cremated in it. The result went against Jeans and the Saints that day, but the coach's achievement in creating a winning culture at St Kilda was extraordinary. When he retired in 1976 his winning percentage as a coach was 58 per cent, and a curse appeared to have lifted from St Kilda.

Jeans didn't mind his reputation as a disciplinarian. During that first press conference as Hawthorn coach, he said as much: "Discipline is an essential ingredient of a team, but once the guidelines are laid down by the coach, there is plenty of room for players to use their initiative within those guidelines." But he bristled at being called defensive: "That's not fair criticism. The defensive label was given to me without any person saying why. If applying pressure and getting involved when you haven't got possession is being defensive, then I am defensive."

Jeans met his players in the Hawthorn Social Club the day after his appointment. John Kennedy Jnr remembers his media-built preconceptions as "a man who loved sucking lemons for fun". Those thoughts were blown away in that first meeting. Jeans began softly, included some touches of humour, part of his trademark knack for storytelling, and then shifted quickly through the oratorical gears. By the end he was shouting, "I will need to earn your respect, and you mine, but I demand you respect this position I hold as the coach! You must respect the position I hold at this football club!"

So began the Jeans era at Hawthorn. Over the next month, he met with his senior players, many of whom would come to regard him as a father figure. One of those meetings was with a 20-year-old Gary Ayres. Injuries and inconsistent form meant Ayres had only played 22 senior games over his first four years, and about the same number in the reserves. To make matters worse, earlier in the year, Ayres' father died in a tractor accident on the family farm, and Ayres was consumed with grief. "Peter Hudson was going back to Glenorchy," Ayres remembers, "and he was looking for players to go back with him to play in the Tassie Football League. I made up my mind I was going to go. The offer was $20,000. I was recently married, I had a young baby, so I went to tell Allan."

Jeans cut straight to the point. "Son, it's the biggest footy mistake you'll make in your life. I'm going to play you. Once you get across that white line it's up to you, but I'll play you." He gave Ayres a deadline. "You've got 24 hours. Tell me at training tomorrow night. I want your answer."

The answer is there in the history books. Eight grand finals, five premierships, a best and fairest award in a premiership year, two Norm Smith Medals, membership of the Australian Football Hall of Fame, Hawthorn Team of the Century.

Gary Ayres decided to stay.

4

A MATTER OF TRUST

In October of 1987 Jeans had been coach of Hawthorn for seven eventful seasons—a period that would come to be known as the club's glory days. He'd won two premierships, steered the team to five consecutive Grand Finals, and two of his players—DiPierdomenico and rover John Platten—became the club's first two Brownlow medallists. Jeans's win-loss record at his second club gleamed at a staggering 124-49, or 71.6%.

But that October was a dark month in this period of sunshine.

For one, the Hawks had just been thrashed in the 1987 Grand Final. On a scorching hot day, arch-rival Carlton dismantled Jeans's men, embarrassed them, in an uncharacteristically listless performance from the men in the brown and gold; worn down by their last gasp preliminary final win over Melbourne a week earlier. It was almost as if the team had been stripped of its superpowers by the novelty of Michael Tuck wearing a sleeveless guernsey. When I ask senior members of the 1989 premiership team about the story of those back-to-back flags of 1988-89, all of them return to 1987.

"We got beaten up a bit that day," says Brereton.

"We were really hurt by that," says Platten.

"We were pretty much shot after the preliminary final," is John Kennedy Jnr's recollection.

In *The Age*, Martin Flanagan put it succinctly: "With the exception of DiPierdomenico, they lacked the desperate excess the occasion required, both physically and mentally. Their chasing appeared calculated, so much so that one wondered if they had been instructed to conserve their energies."

Hawthorn was exhausted on Grand Final day. Carlton's reward for winning the qualifying final against Hawthorn was avoiding a preliminary final against Melbourne on the vast expanses of VFL Park at Waverley. It was a bizarre game, if only for the meteorological fact that the wind did a 180-degree turn at quarter-time. For three quarters the Hawks ran the ball against the wind, hanging tough, and eventually stole victory when mercurial forward Gary Buckenara famously kicked a goal after the siren. A week later, 35-degree temperatures were not exactly made-to-order for the leg-weary Hawks.

Full-forward Jason Dunstall missed the 1987 Grand Final with a sprained ankle. Brereton was enduring a season of back pain, treated with monthly epidurals and a brace, and also suffered a crack through the middle of the ball joint of the ankle (talus) that needed reconstructive surgery in the post season. His opponent, David Rhys-Jones kept him to six kicks and no goals and won the Norm Smith Medal. "I wasn't in showroom condition, but I was out there. I should have done better," says Brereton. For Jeans it was a second blown attempt in four years at achieving the club's first back-to-back flags.

But there was a more serious speed-hump ahead. At the Hawthorn under-19s best and fairest night a few weeks later, Jeans complained to his wife Mary of dizziness and a headache. Thankfully, he left the function and went to hospital, where it was determined he'd suffered a burst blood vessel at the base of the brain. This was serious stuff. Forty per cent of people who suffer ruptured aneurysms die from them.

Fifteen per cent of those afflicted don't make it to hospital, and 66 per cent accrue permanent neurological deficit. Despite it being a "difficult site for surgery", Jeans's surgeon sealed the burst vessel with a steel clip, and it was a best-case result. Jeans could expect to make a full recovery, with next to no lasting symptoms.

Jeans was, in those months, a man feeling the strain. He was recently retired from the police force, and 1987 was only his second year as a full-time VFL coach—a move prompted by the disappointment of the back-to-back Grand Final losses to Essendon in 1984-85, and vindicated by Hawthorn's crushing victory over the Blues in the 1986 decider. Jeans had received his financial benefits after long years of dedicated police service, and he'd received them at exactly the wrong moment. The October share market crash hit many investors hard, and Jeans was particularly affected. Those losses compounded his rough treatment at the hands of cash-strapped St Kilda, where Jeans was among the seven unsecured creditors who chose to accept as little as 22.5 cents on the dollar in 1984 for unpaid wages dating back to the early 1970s, so that the club could live on. "He was under a lot of personal pressure," Hawthorn's champion full-back Chris Langford recalls.

Jeans's doctors ordered him to take a year off footy, to de-stress and ensure his healing and recuperation. After 12 months of rest, *if* Jeans felt fit enough, he could resume.

There were two men in line to assume the caretaker role. One was Des Meagher, the 1971 premiership wingman who sat on match committee and coached the reserves. Meagher was tough, laconic, wiry. He spoke with a slow drawl and a dry honesty. I remember him calling me in after I made a mistake at training during my one season on the senior list. He said, "Willo, you can't kick, you can't run, you can't jump, you can't handball—you can mark, *but you're not even doing that at the moment!*" So that was Des. Clean living, straight talking, hard running, and so, so competitive. There's a famous story from John Origlasso, a reserves player of my vintage, that Meagher suffered a minor stroke on the club's regular Kew Boulevard run and continued back to Glenferrie, undaunted. "I was beaten home by a bloke twice my age who'd suffered a mild stroke," Origlasso grins. The story lost much of its lustre when Des suffered a much larger stroke twenty years later. May he rest in peace.

The other candidate was Alan Joyce. Joyce played 49 games in the ruck for Hawthorn in the mostly dark years between the club's first flag in 1961 and its wooden spoon in 1965. That he'd done it while standing only 185 centimetres said something for his courage and his ability to get the best out of himself. After his VFL career finished, he captain-coached Preston to back-to-back VFA flags in 1968-69 and East Fremantle to a WAFL Grand Final in 1977. In 1986 he returned to Melbourne for work reasons and Jeans made him his forward scout, watching the team Hawthorn would play the following week. An unusual quirk of the fixture meant he saw Carlton 17 times that season, hours in which he gained important insights. Jeans later credited Joyce with helping to dismantle the Blues in the 1986 Grand Final, which Hawthorn won by 42 points.

In 1987 Joyce rose from forward scout to football manager at Hawthorn. He was organised, efficient and club-minded. He wasn't a small talker, a backslapper, or a smiler. I remember in my first week as a listed player, by which time Joyce was coach, I started a sentence with "Joycey, may I…" and he stuck a finger in my chest and said, "Look, the name's Alan. Let's get that right for starters." DiPierdomenico tells a story in Michael and Harry Gordon's *One for All* (Wilkinson Publishing, 2009) about the difference between Joyce as the club's football manager, and his predecessor, Tony Farrugia:

"When Tony was football manager we'd walk into his office, say, 'What's going on, Tony?', to pass the time of day. His table was messy. I remember saying, 'Oh, Knightsy's getting that much is he?' When Joycey took over I walked in and noticed his desk was very neat … He said, 'What can I do for you?' I told him I just came in as a matter of course, nothing special, just for conversation. 'Well don't bother coming in any more like that,' he said."

There was no off switch to Joyce's intensity, but people knew where they stood with him and his lengthy coaching apprenticeship spelled out his qualities. He was wholeheartedly committed to the "Hawthorn Football Club"— always referred to deferentially by Joyce, always in that expanded, three-word formulation.

During a bedside meeting at Jeans's Cheltenham home, Joyce was anointed as caretaker. In that room, famously, the two made a deal, as Jeans recalled to Michael Gordon in *One For All*: "I told him I had two previous chances to win two in a row and each time I'd missed out. I said if he could take the flag in 1988, I'd go back-to-back with him in 1989. It was more than a bargain. It was more like a pact, a matter of trust."

5

EXTRA VOLATILITY

The Jeans-built Hawthorn team of the eighties was so dominant, so bejewelled with talent across every line, that Alan Joyce is sometimes unfairly painted as a straw coach, a leader in name only. But many of his senior players refute this.

"There are a lot of great teams that don't win premierships," says Brereton. "He was a new voice," says Ayres. "The blokes loved Joycey," says Platten (and yes, I can't help but note that the best rover of the 1980s is allowed to call him Joycey). "I really enjoyed him as a person and a voice," says Langford. "He was a very good judge of a footballer."

On the first day of pre-season training in 1988, on the sports fields of Trinity Grammar School, Bulleen, Joyce addressed the players. He spoke about the 1987 Grand Final disaster and how the focus of his one season in charge would be toughness. "We'll never get punched up by an opponent in a Grand Final again!" he glared, his dark eyes blazing and his sharp finger pointing. Training that night began with half an hour of boxing.

Brereton was one who appreciated what he calls "the extra volatility" that Joyce encouraged. Brereton, too, was haunted by the 1987 Grand Final result; his direct opponent had won the Norm Smith Medal, and he still believes the Hawks were rag-dolled by the Blues from the opening bounce. As Brereton said on SEN's *Crunch Time* pre-game program in 2016:

"I stood on the line at centre half-forward and I looked over and there was Ian Aitkin and Peter Dean and they had ganged up on Russell Morris and he was backing away, arms up, trying to fend off half-slap hits that might get you $1500 fines now. I looked across and normally I'd have just gone over there and done something. But I looked over and thought, 'I'm a bit banged up over here, I've got my own fight to battle away at.' And to this day, the one thing I regret about that day is not going over there and bashing one of them, because I think that might have changed a little bit of mindset."

In 1988 Joyce didn't condone violence that sat outside the game's Laws. "He'd tell us to give it to them, but not to get suspended" says Brereton, who went and got suspended anyway—a six-week holiday for striking St Kilda's Danny Frawley in round 10.

On the eve of Brereton's round 17 return, with media cameras trained on Glenferrie Oval, Joyce started training by handing his star the ball and saying, "Right Dermie, let's go." On game day, go he did, marauding through the centre of the ground at the first bounce and picking off Melbourne's Dean Chiron with a bone-rattling shirtfront. A minute later, strutting around at centre half-forward, his permed locks as voluminous as they'd ever be, and his Speedo-like shorts so small as to defy belief, Brereton had kicked the first of his four goals for the day and Hawthorn was on its way to a 69-point win in the top-of-the-ladder clash. With one brutal, decisive action, Brereton had set the afternoon on its course.

Better was to come a week later at the same ground. Brereton, now shod in lime green boots, created some folklore when he charged through Essendon's three-quarter time huddle, cannoning into his opponent Bill Duckworth and another Dons backman, Dean

Wallis. "I felt like telling my players not to worry about Dermott," Essendon coach Kevin Sheedy told reporters later. "He's just another mad Irishman." Either calming them, or perhaps sensing a chance to channel the energy of the moment, Joyce separated his players from even the Hawks trainers, and after the coach's final address they backed up Brereton's act of provocation by turning a slender four-point lead at that final change into a 26-point win. Afterwards, in *The Herald*, praise for Brereton's "terrific" approach to roughhousing opponents came from the man who'd spent the previous decade wearing Hawthorn's No.23 guernsey, Don Scott, but his approving nod came with a prophetic rejoinder: "Of course, sooner or later someone is going to come after him and try to knock him off."

This openly confrontational Hawthorn was becoming a hallmark of Joyce's temporary reign. "Rather than quell the aggression he [Joyce] fostered it," Brereton says. "With Jeansy it was always, 'Stay away from that, you'll get reported, you'll miss weeks', whereas Joycey gave us our head."

"It was combative, and it sharpened us up," says Kennedy.

"More disciplined, and more of a focus on being physical and aggressive," says Langford. In *The Herald*, Caroline Wilson observed another of Hawthorn's most visible traits, its togetherness: "When Joyce calls his players into a circle, they huddle so close that a rabbit couldn't sneak through."

If Joyce had encouraged aggression on the field, there was also the occasional hostility he brought to his human interactions. Among the players, the most infamous of these moments was when Joyce pushed Chris Mew in the chest. By 1988 Mew was an eleven-year veteran and a two-time premiership player. A quiet, mustachioed centre half-back who curbed the best players in the game, week in week out, he was fazed by nothing and no-one. "I'd done my hamstring," Mew remembers. "He [Joyce] was going off about something and he shoved me right in the middle of the chest. I told him to get fucked because I wasn't going to put up with that. Then he kind of backed off, and that was it."

"He was always angry and always tense at training," Platten says, "and he didn't tell too many jokes, wasn't dry like Jeansy. He wasn't as *pleasant* as Jeansy… He was a great football manager, a great coach, but more tense than Allan Jeans was."

Kennedy remembers the altercation with Mew. "Alan, he was ferocious. I got on well with him, but he was very combative, a lot of confrontation. That was his way though, and like him or hate him, he was the coach and I always respected the position he held."

The results were phenomenal. Hawthorn lost only three games in the 22-round home and away season and finished with a percentage of 142.3%. Even watching them train left an impression on the football press. The Thursday before Hawthorn's semi-final win over Carlton, *The Sun's* Bruce Matthews sat in the stands at Glenferrie and marvelled at the precision of each training drill, the pack mentality, the sheer repetition of perfection. "Watching the squad of 25 players sprint in the same direction to a single point was an awesome sight," Matthews wrote the next day. "… like a bushfire funnelling air to feed the flame."

In the feverish build-up to the '88 Grand Final, Joyce claimed the Hawks were "keeping a normal profile", which in his case was certainly true. Looking for photo opportunities, the Press asked him to hold the premiership Cup with his opposite number, John Northey, and the answer was a polite but firm no. Okay Alan, can you just shake his hand for the cameras? Again: no. On game day, the hottest of hot favourites, the Hawks kicked 22.20 and demolished Melbourne by a then record 96 points. For his 10 commanding marks and five goals, Brereton won not only a premiership medallion, but the benefits of another hare-brained Lou Richards bet: Hawthorn's win meant the TV personality would scrub Brereton's red Ferrari clean with a cotton ball on the steps of the Hawthorn Town Hall.

The outlook was less rosy for the rest of the football world. "By and large the competition was terrified of playing Hawthorn," Brereton says. Both he and Ayres regard the 1988 team as the strongest they played in. Generally, the '88 Hawks enter calculations when it comes to those futile debates on which is the greatest team of all time.

With so many guns in their absolute prime, Joyce gave his stars plenty of rein. "Joycey did a really good job but he didn't rock the boat," says Peter Schwab. "It was business as usual." "We literally coached ourselves," says Brereton, but then quickly credits Joyce for trusting and empowering his players and allowing it to happen. "I've heard David Parkin speak about the (Carlton) 1995 team. He says one of the best things he ever did was to say, 'Here you go guys, coach yourselves'."

There was even some talk that Joyce might keep the job for 1989. Both Gary Linnell in *The Age* and Geoff Poulter in *The Herald* wrote Jeans-has-nothing-left-to-prove articles for their newspapers. During the Foster's World Cup post-season trip to London and Toronto—where the Hawks would be led for the last time by Joyce—Lou Richards approached Hawthorn's chairman of selectors Brian Coleman with his 'whispers'. "I'm hearing things, Brian, I'm hearing Joycey's got the job."

Coleman's reply was emphatic: "No, *Yabby's* got the job."

Internally, there was never any doubt. The players loved Jeans, and they were looking forward to his return.

It should also be said that Joyce was a man of his word—a man of Hawthorn and for Hawthorn. He never campaigned to keep the job he must have coveted. He rejected offers from other clubs. He wouldn't sit on the club's match committee in 1989, allowing Jeans the space that Jeans allowed him. When 1988 was done and dusted, the flag secured, Joyce quietly returned to the role of football manager, to that tidy desk that was not open to Dipper for casual chats. As Jeans said to Michael Gordon: "He did not want to do anything that could be considered rocking the boat. Only his wife Rhonda and I would fully understand the sacrifice he made."

On the night of the 1988 premiership, Joyce stood up at the Hilton Hotel and thanked his players. Visibly relieved, he finally let the mask slip, cracking what might have been his only joke of the year: "John

Kennedy (Snr) taught me to say nothing and Allan Jeans taught me to say less." Recalling his bedside pact with Jeans, Joyce then confirmed what Hawthorn people had known all along: Jeans would coach the Hawks in 1989. Soon afterwards, a photographer caught the two men in a far more candid scene than the photo opportunities Joyce had avoided days earlier: passing a seated Jeans on his way back from the podium, Joyce, the apprentice, placed his trusting hands on the master's shoulders—a comfortable but typically modest display of fraternity and respect. At the club's 1988 annual general meeting Jeans made his public reply: "He has finished his part of the bargain. Now it's my turn."

6

FROM WHY TO HOW

The Geelong players were boozing in Toronto when they met their new coach, Malcolm Blight. They'd just played a post-season exhibition match at the Toronto Skydome, the footy was done, and Blight had completed his commentary duties with Channel Seven.

Veteran defender Damian Drum, later to become coach of Fremantle and later a Victorian MP—in state and federal parliaments—says that right from that first meeting, Blight showed good leadership. "I think he only stayed about five minutes. He saw we were up and about, and he decided that it wasn't the right place for him to be. That's classic good judgment right there. If you're an incoming coach, don't engage with blokes on a footy trip!"

"We'd all had a few beers," Darren Flanigan grins. "Blighty is a good person to hang out with socially. Of course, it was all very different once training began."

As a coach, Blight was renowned for devising gruelling pre-season training regimes. When he returned to Woodville in 1983 the club was at a low ebb. As Blight says, "They'd won one game. In a ten-team competition they were probably fifteenth!" He was alarmed when more than 50 players turned up to the first night of training, an unwieldy number. Blight set them a task: "Run around this oval. If you stop before I tell you to, open that gate over there and keep going. We don't need you back here." At the other end of his coaching career—those ill-fated 15 games at St Kilda in 2000—Blight created angst with his "no balls" policy at pre-season. He thought the Saints were unfit, and he planned to fix it. They wouldn't touch the Sherrins until January.

In the scorching hot pre-season of 1989, the Geelong players invested sweat and lactic acid in what they hoped was a new beginning. "To say that we trained hard, it was almost a flog," says Blight. "One thing you can do as a coach is eliminate fitness (as an issue) ... I wouldn't let them touch the footys until I knew that they were hard enough." The players quickly got a sense that the workload was not negotiable. On the first night of pre-season, Blight outlined the agenda—5 x 2000m runs—and asked if there was anyone who couldn't do it to the best of his ability. Bruce 'The Prez' Lindner, who had beautiful footy skills and a self- confidence to match his nickname, raised a hand. "I've just come back from San Fran," he said. "I'm jetlagged." Lindner completed the session with the reserves group. He didn't play his first senior game for the season until round seven.

As Blight cracked the whip on the track, he laid down "The Rules" off it. The Rules was a three-page document he took to each footy club he coached, as a simple but detailed outline of what a Blight-led team must do. Some of the rules related to on-field actions. They were devised to make each of Blight's players predictable to his teammates. For example, under pressure, every player was required to kick it to the centre half-forward area, so Geelong's forwards would know fractionally before their opponents where the ball was going. Marking from behind was okay, as long as the ball spilled forwards if a mark was not taken. Keep the ball in front. Move the ball forwards. You could kick a torpedo, so long as you were proficient in a skill which had been all but outlawed by a number of League coaches. If you mucked up your torpedo, you had to resort to drop punts. There was even a rule that gave players three chances. The first mistake might have been your bad luck. The second mistake might have been your opponent's good luck. But the third mistake, watch out!

Behind all the on-field rules sat the overriding philosophy, the one that had been outlined to the Geelong Board: *the aim of the game is to score goals quickly*. Blight loved what he called 'the double switch'— quick ball movement to runners in space. He hated forwards leading to the boundary line. Mark Yeates says that one time, late in his career, he thought he was playing well, but at three-quarter time Blight accosted him: "If you don't start running off and getting possessions you'll be dropped!" Says Yeates: "I thought this was a bit hard to take, so might have given him a bit of lip, and sure enough he was right. First time in my life I played in the seconds."

There were off-field rules too. It was decreed, for example, that players could not talk to the coach about being dropped until the Monday after. "Otherwise you spend an inordinate amount of time on player number 21, who's going to play in the twos," Blight explains. "Whinging and not turning up was instant dismissal."

Blight was a mesmerising presence, right from the first meeting. "I could have listened to him all day," says Geelong defender Tim Darcy. "We loved him," Brownless told James Button in *Comeback: The fall and rise of Geelong* (Melbourne University Press, 2016).

"In that first year he was incredibly positive," says Drum. "Even after a loss, he'd come out full of positivity."

"He was a brilliant speaker," says Yeates. "He had instant presence and he reached everyone in the room—boot-studders, staff, players. He talked about the hard things in footy, the things that take no skill. He really changed my life."

The other thing Blight could do was *teach*. Television audiences got a taste of it during his commentary stints in 1988, and also in his 'Blight on Tactics' newspaper columns in *The Age*. In 1989, and at the start of every one of his seasons as a senior coach, he'd do a refresher on how to hold, kick, mark and handball the footy. Everyone was invited, including trainers. "I enjoy the technique of football," Blight explains. "A baby doesn't come out of the womb able to kick a footy. In those days, kids were mainly taught by dads and teachers, and not every dad was a great technique player, and not every teacher was a great technique teacher."

Blight estimates that in 1989 half the players in the VFL and SANFL did not possess the basic footy techniques.

Drum believes Blight was a true pioneer. "He was the first coach who started actually teaching blokes how to play," he says. "Before Malcolm arrived, the great coaches were mainly motivators, men who harnessed effort and appealed to emotion: 'We've got to win because we hate this mob' ... 'These blokes have got our spot in the finals ....' Remember what happened last time!' ... that sort of thing. Blight was the first coach who'd actually say to you, 'When you play on this bloke he has no right foot' or, 'This bloke spoils with his right hand' or 'This bloke is no good in the wet'. He taught you how you could be better. He transformed it from *why* we should win to *how* we are going to win."

Lindner says Blight's football lessons transformed his game. "I'd been playing football since I was a young kid, and he taught me things that I wish I had have known much, much earlier. Like in my role as a half-forward flanker ... When the ball was kicked towards a contest it was more of a guess, which side I'd run to. With Malcolm, we did crumbing drills with competitive players going for the mark, and he pointed out that 75 per cent of balls for a right-handed spoil go in the 9-12 o'clock quadrant, as you face the ball. A lot of his teaching was on the lines of percentage—that you get a greater chance to get the ball if you run to the right spot. That was a big one for me. It would have added 20 per cent disposals and opportunities."

Blight had fallen in love with the analytical side of footy, even as a player. Because Ron Casey led Channel Seven in the 1970s and was a North supporter and future chairman, he allowed Ron Barassi's men access to the studios to watch footage. "We'd go in on a Thursday night, have a meal, and watch either us, or our opposition that week. Coming from Adelaide I'd never seen that, that you can actually learn football from a video ... something inside of me loved it. I couldn't get enough of it."

By 1989 video was a little more accessible and Blight was sitting up after every game, long into the night, reviewing the tape and making copious notes. "I never asked anyone else to do it. Now they [head coaches] have got five or six blokes to help do it." Blight laments that he was a smoker back then, and that "cigarettes and a little bottle of port" fortified him as he reviewed the games into the small hours of Sunday morning. "I had to know the reason we won or lost, and I'd find out what I did wrong, and then what we could do to help out the players."

If he's painted in footy history as a left-field thinker who succeeded with unconventional methods, it also pays to respect the preparation and scholarship that informed Blight's coaching philosophy. That and his psychological hold over the men tasked with following his blueprint. Says Lindner: "If I was starting my new team, I'd have him as my first coach, but I think he'd also have a 'use by' date on him at clubs. And I don't think you can berate and manipulate players to the extent now that you could back then."

7

A NEW DIET

In 1989 Hawthorn's pre-season training program ran five nights a week. It was exhausting, an ordeal to be survived, endured. "I was always just so relieved to get through pre-season," Ayres remembers. "You've got a full-time job, a young family...it was such a time management issue...you'd be out doing the road runs, and the temperature would be 30 degrees with another five or 10 degrees beaming off the road."

Monday, Wednesday and Friday sessions took place on the track at Glenferrie—brown training jumpers versus gold ones, lane work, fartlek running, 'random ball' (a multidirectional version of circle-work—non-contact but taking place across the full ground to simulate match conditions). If Jeans didn't like what he saw, he'd send stragglers off to 'Brumby Hill', a small incline under the scoreboard which had risen from the Merri Creek mud with the clear purpose of hurting footballers. On Tuesdays and Thursdays, it was running in groups. Players could select their pain: Kew Boulevard, The Tan, the fairways of Wattle Park, or 12 kilometres of beachside running down at

Sandringham and Black Rock.

"Yabby used to go to that one," former Hawks on-baller Dean Anderson recalls, "because he lived down that way. He'd be hiding in the ti-tree watching you!"

This was the dawn of professionalism in footy. At the end of 1987, Joyce, then football manager, responded to Hawthorn's lethargic showing in the Grand Final by poaching Karen Inge, a dietician, from Collingwood. "Karen, you and I are the only two new things at this club," Joyce told her, "and there is only one way we can go." Inge made a real difference, teaching players about hydration and cutting out excesses of alcohol, fat and fast food. Skinfold measurements were a new concept in footy, and the players were competitive, though not in the way Inge hoped. Anderson laughs: "Blokes would come in and have a competition as to who had put on the *most* weight over summer and celebrate that!"

Inge had her work cut out when it came to tempering the more-than-traditional, closer-to-sacred Thursday night fry-ups in the trainers' room. Players dropped in for a sausage, a cup of hot chips and maybe two or three dim sims for good measure, all washed down with a paper cup full of Coke. I remember head trainer Bobby Yeomans' jelly belly shaking with derision when Inge successfully lobbied to have them serve pineapple. Times were-a-changing. Ayres says Inge helped him lose five kilograms in 1988, which aided him in his perennial battle against soft tissue injuries.

Inge changed the fitness culture at Hawthorn for years to come, but other players weren't quite as diligent as Ayres. When Paul Cooper returned from his holidays looking decidedly porky in the pre-season of 1993, it was no laughing matter. Joyce made him run the Kew Boulevard wearing a full-length fleecy tracksuit from the 1970s, "one of the old fluffy yellow ones with 'Wynvale' written across the front," says Cooper. When he failed to return within the prescribed time, he was sent out to do it again. Joyce banned Cooper from training until he lost the excess weight. "He made me do boxing in the sauna," says

Cooper. "I asked Karen Inge if this was doing me any good and she said, 'None at all. When you get home make sure you drink five litres of water'." Cooper can laugh now. "I was pretty fat. I'd had a hernia operation. I remember Langers' total skinfolds for all six sites was equal to my stomach."

For my part—and it was a very small part—Karen Inge convinced me to cut down on cheese toasties.

8

RUNNING OUT OF TIME

The neon-lit problem for Malcolm Blight and his "my rules, no exceptions" revolution at Kardinia Park can be summarised in two words: Gary Ablett.

Ablett was always the exception. He was an exception to what a human body could physically achieve on a footy field. He was also an exception to what a regular player was expected to do off it.

In the first two weeks of pre-season 1989 Ablett didn't turn up to training.

Jeans had a first-hand appreciation of what Geelong's new coach was going through. Ablett had joined his older brothers, Geoff and Kevin at Hawthorn just before the Jeans era began. From day one, his natural gifts were obvious. DiPierdomenico saw a young Gary at a pre-season session at Box Hill athletics track. The team was running 100-metre sprints. "Gary beat his brothers Kevin and Geoff by three metres. We thought, 'What? That can't be right?'" Geoff Ablett played in 202 games and two premierships for the Hawks and won the Grand Final sprint a record four times—decent going, considering he couldn't compete for the three years he was playing in the main event. Geoff was generally regarded as the 'fastest man in boots'. Kevin was lightning-fast too. Gary, it seemed, was quicker.

David Parkin remembers these races too: "To see a race with Geoff, Kevin and Gary involved was quite incredible. They would all be metres ahead of everyone else and would be laughing as one beat the other."

The difficulty was introducing the younger Abletts to the disciplines of big League footy. Kevin and Gary loved country life—fishing for trout and shooting rabbits. In his letter to the Hawthorn Board dated 7 September 1980, Parkin wrote a one-sentence review: "The two Abletts, Kevin and Gary, appear destined not to become Hawthorn players."

John Kennedy Jnr remembers Gary's Hawthorn days: "I played a few games with Gary Snr … yeah, when he played, when he turned up! They'd bring him in from Drouin … I had the number 34 locker and he had 36. He was a nice fella. You could see he had the talent, but he was all over the shop at the time. He was either in trouble at Drouin, so they couldn't get him down, or he wouldn't get to training. I think Gary would be the first to admit that he was very difficult to manage back then."

"It was a waste," says Ayres of Ablett's Hawthorn years. Ayres actually played with Gary even earlier, in the Drouin under 12s and under 14s. Ayres's father, the local policeman, was the coach. "I remember the day Gary asked to play for us, but said he'd like a dollar a game." Ayres laughs. 'The old man said, 'I've got that many kids lining up to play, Gary, you won't be getting a dollar a game'." A few years later, Ablett was dominating Gippsland senior football as a 15-year-old. A local businessman paid him $10 a goal.

Ablett didn't have a driver's licence and was living with a group of bikies in Fawkner during his time with the Hawks. Football manager Tony Farrugia would turn up on his doorstep and drive him to training. "It was a 45-minute drive from Hawthorn," Farrugia told

The Age's Caroline Wilson in 1989. "I used to say to him, 'Gary, if you're good at one thing, you're good at footy but you're running out of time.' He knew he was blessed, but he couldn't make it at city life."

Peter Curran played reserves footy with Ablett in 1982, "Even then, he was the best footballer I'd seen. The things he could do," Curran says. Peter Schwab agrees: "We used to laugh at what he did. Those of us in the seconds knew he had that much talent he should have been playing firsts. In 1982 he played the last game of the year at Princes Park and I think he kicked three. We expected him to play finals in 1982 with the seniors, but he got dropped and came back to the seconds. That was probably the wrong decision. He never fronted again, and we never saw him again till he bobbed up at Geelong."

Jeans lost patience with Gary at the end of 1982. Their rapport had never been strong, the career policeman struggling with a talented kid who'd had his run ins with the law. But the real disciplinary issues were football ones. "He wasn't going to put up with it anymore," remembers Ayres. "I think the club had done a lot in terms of organising lifts to and from Hawthorn, and maybe fishing and shooting were a little more important for Gary than playing footy."

In 1983 Ablett played at Myrtleford in the Ovens and Murray League, in the picturesque alpine territory near Bright, and created bush footy legends that will be murmured down the generations. He was Gary Ablett, after all, and he did Gary Ablett-type things, no matter that they were only witnessed by a smattering of passionate locals and a ring of honking cars. In the first semi-final, his team trailing by 22 points with five minutes to go, Ablett booted two, gave two away, and Myrtleford pinched the game. "It was the most scintillating five minutes of football I've ever seen, and I was part of it," his captain-coach Greg Nicholls told Caroline Wilson.

Bush tales of superhuman skill reached Cats powerbroker Bill Goggin and coach Tom Hafey at Geelong during 1983, and the club made Ablett an offer. Contractually speaking he was still a Hawthorn player, and with the bush telegraph working overtime to raise Ablett's value, the Hawks drove a hard bargain. After some haggling Geelong paid Hawthorn a $60,000 clearance fee. In his first game for Geelong, Ablett produced a performance that served as a microcosm of his enigmatic career to that point: three goals, 20 disposals and a place in the umpire's report book for striking Fitzroy's Garry Wilson, the latter earning him a three-week suspension. In his ninth game for the Cats he booted five goals from 30 touches. At the end of that first season he was Geelong's best and fairest from just 15 games.

Ablett shone from the outset. But he was still the same complicatedand enigmatic talent that had perplexed and frustrated Jeans and the Hawthorn hierarchy. Successive Geelong coaches—Hafey and John Devine—struggled with him, constantly re-drawing lines in the sand, a leniency that became more fraught as Ablett's body matured, and his performances became more and more extraordinary, if somewhat inconsistent.

The rest of the players gradually accepted that there was one set of rules for them, and another for Ablett. Looking back on Ablett's first four years at the club, his captain of that time, Mick Turner, would tell Ablett biographer Ken Piesse that Hafey, with his different rules for special players, made a rod for Devine's back. An old-school disciplinarian, Devine's time as coach also coincided awkwardly with Ablett's fervent embrace of the Christian faith, which had the benefit of tempering the star player's previously wild social life but re-ordered his priorities in ways that didn't always align with his coach's plans. For one, he flatly refused to train on Sundays, attending church instead.

An example of Ablett-related rule-bending that sticks with many of the Geelong players came in 1986, Devine's first year as coach. Approaching an Anzac Day clash with North Melbourne in round five, Devine's Cats were 0-4, battling away without the services of Greg Williams, Bernard Toohey and David Bolton—all pre-season departures to Sydney—and their talisman Ablett, injured and seemingly still weeks away from his return.

Contrary to the myth that he never turned up if he wasn't playing,

Ablett took his place in the stands in advance of the match, sitting beside his brother Geoff, but popped off for a while to head down into the rooms and say hello to his teammates. It had already been a strange afternoon; Geelong's game was the second in an MCG double-header that day, with Sydney having just defeated Melbourne in the 2pm game. The next time Geoff Ablett saw his brother, he was running onto the field in the blue and white hoops for the twilight game.

Gary Ablett may have been aloof; stories were already legion of his inability to remember the names of teammates outside Geelong's top ten stars—but he was not immune to the pre-game buzz and the smell of liniment. In the bowels of the MCG that day, he took a quick look around and suddenly felt in the mood. He immediately approached Devine, asking to be slipped into the team as the latest of late inclusions. It was selfish, Turner thought, and not the kind of thing a club like Hawthorn would tolerate. For Devine, it was a serious dilemma.

Linder recalls: "A guy named Craig Evans was playing his first game at the MCG. He had his parents down and everything … John came to a couple of the senior players, myself included and said, 'What do I do? Do I play him?' I said, 'It's not my call, you've got to make the decision John'."

Other senior players, Terry Bright and Peter Johnston among them, petitioned for Ablett. Faced with the choice of disappointing an expectant rookie [Evans had played his first two games in the smaller suburban environs of Windy Hill and Victoria Park] or putting his superstar off-side from day one, Devine went with Ablett. Evans and his parents—and as the tale has evolved down the decades, the carloads of friends have turned into busloads—had their big moment postponed. Wearing hastily arranged gear, Ablett kicked 3.2 from nine possessions and Geelong lost by 62 points. Turner still fumes about it. Craig Evans played seven more games for the Cats before being shipped off to the Brisbane Bears at the end of the year—not long enough for Gary Ablett to learn his name.

Then there was the time a Geelong official approached Devine and told him that if he even considered dropping Ablett, he would, "have a queue of people a mile long outside the club, wanting to pull it down brick by brick." When Ablett did show up for training, Devine could only hold his attention by creating training activities with a competitive element.

When Devine lost the Geelong coaching job at the end of the 1988 season, he spent a few quiet months back in his native Hobart, stewing on his demise, wondering how, having steered a team full of potential, and with the League's most obviously gifted player at his disposal, he couldn't once lead Geelong to the finals.

In November that year Devine admitted to *The Sun's* Geoff McClure that the club had been right to make its move, and finally talked about his fractious relationship with Ablett, who'd threatened to quit the club in 1987 over indiscreet comments Devine made to a newspaper reporter when Ablett pulled out of another game, citing lethargy. It took a lot of convincing on behalf of club and coach to get Ablett back once a frustrated Devine let rip. "In the end, we worked out a compromise and Gary returned," Devine told McClure. "But I knew then that I had lost Ablett as the player I knew he could be. I knew he had lost trust in me." This was the conundrum Blight inherited from his predecessors. To bring that conundrum into sharp focus, Ablett didn't attend the first two weeks of pre-season training before the 1989 season. Blight picked up the phone: "Gary I need to talk to you. I want to meet you at a place called Balyang Sanctuary."

9

THE BRIDGE

There's a bridge spanning the waters of Geelong's Balyang Sanctuary, a few kilometres from Kardinia Park. It is fenced by treated pine posts, spaced with black metal bars, and reeds peak through from the inky waters beneath. The park is tranquil and picturesque, with beautiful gumtrees standing tall as the Barwon ebbs and flows.

When Ablett arrived for his meeting with Blight, Geelong's new coach took him to the middle of the bridge. There they stopped, two of the most brilliant footballers ever to play, one now the coach, the other the key to Geelong's fortunes in 1989 and beyond.

They talked about training. Blight himself didn't love training hard in his early days. "I wasn't an A-Grade trainer to start with. I was probably in the B-Grade really," he says. "I did enough to get by. I just loved playing. It took a while for me until the penny dropped." They talked footy—about Blight's attacking vision, the key role Ablett could play, the strengths of his game, how he could improve his consistency. They talked about the difference between ability and talent. "Ability is what your parents gave you—short, tall, quick, slow," Blight says. "Talent is understanding what to do with that ability." Then Blight issued his famous mid-bridge ultimatum: "Gary, you either walk across here, and you go home and get your bag and you come to training, or you piss off." It's a famous story, and Blight has told it many times. "It was the whole symbolic thing," he says. "Walk across with me or I'm gonna push you off."

Lindner says that he was taken to the bridge too. "Same bridge, same ultimatum...not that anyone cares. It's not quite the same as Gary Ablett walking across the bridge, is it? But it does make you wonder. How many players did Malcolm take to the bridge?"

Ablett went home and got his gear. Not only did he come to training, but Blight made him stay afterwards, running 200s and 400s until he couldn't walk. "That was a rude awakening for everyone at the footy club," Blight says. "The player with the most ability, and I just flogged him. I made him catch up the work he missed."

Would Blight have sacked Ablett if he'd answered differently on the bridge? Blight says he would have and given the equanimity with which he later accepted Ablett's short-lived retirement in February 1991, you tend to believe him. "You can't threaten to push them off the bridge and not push them off the bridge," he says.

Drum reinforces this position. He remembers the training session before the Balyang confrontation, a Friday before Christmas, and what Blight said to the rest of the playing group. Recalls Drum, "Malcolm said, 'Regarding Ablett, he's not here. It's compulsory to be here. He will be here on Monday or he's not playing for us'." I know as a coach, when you say these sort of things, you always give yourself an opportunity for an out, but there was absolutely no wriggle room in the wording he used. 'He'll be here on Monday or he won't be playing for us this year.' I was really impressed. He meant it and I'm sure he would have followed through."

But Blight's issues with Ablett, the exception, were not all resolved. The Balyang meeting did not change Ablett's personality. He didn't suddenly crave discipline and structure. And whatever his shortfalls on the training track, Ablett's strengths were so freakish that there was always that temptation to accommodate him. Even Jeans, sacker of Ablett in '82, frustrated to the point of abandonment, *re-recruited* Gary Ablett, signing him to a five-year deal at the end of 1987, when Ablett fell out with Devine. It was only because Ablett reneged on the Hawthorn contract—worth north of $100,000, divided between playing duties and a day job with a cleaning company—before the end of the cooling off period that he remained a Cat.

The bridge meeting drew Ablett back to training. For most of 1989 he had a strong attendance record. The exception was the Sunday morning recovery sessions. Blight had made these compulsory, but the now deeply religious Ablett was missing them to attend church. Blight called together his captain Damian Bourke, vice-captain Mark Bairstow and four or five senior players to the Kardinia Park coach's room. "What do you reckon boys?" he asked. "Gary's beliefs; they're taking him to church on a Sunday, which prevents him training here with us. I'll finish him! We'll finish him up right now if it doesn't work for the rest of the group."

The meeting took place on Sunday 28 May 1989. The day before, against Richmond, Ablett had kicked 14.2, after starting on the wing, in a 134-point victory. When Richmond's Brendan Bower trotted over to become one of Ablett's five hapless opponents that day, the Geelong star grinned and greeted him: "How are you goin', mate?"

"In the end it was a unanimous decision," Blight smiles. "We'd let him go to church on Sundays."

10

WONDER COACH

Hawthorn and Geelong met only once in the regular season of 1989—the famous round six clash at Princes Park. "It was a clinker of a game," Blight says. "Almost a forerunner."

Hawthorn went in having won four of its first five games, which surprised nobody. The loss had come against Collingwood in round one. Geelong started the season 3-2, kicking plenty of goals but suffering the narrowest of defeats against Fitzroy and North Melbourne—by one and two points respectively.

Blight was particularly furious after the Fitzroy loss at Princes Park in round five. The Cats had been 32 points up at three-quarter time and lost on the siren. "I had a sense we were starting to freewheel a bit," Blight remembers. In the post-game meeting, he called everyone in ("Players, officials, reserves, basically the whole club," says Tim Darcy) and gave them a dressing-down. "We need to consider where we are heading as an organisation!" Blight fumed. And for the players, Blight's sermon finished ominously: "Right, mouthguards on Monday—it ain't going to be easy."

On Monday, some nervous Cats sat in front of a blackboard, waiting for Blight to write down the night's painful prescription. Blight was a meticulous coach and drills were always written on the board at the start of the night. That night there were three words on the blackboard: "DON'T GET CHANGED."

"We were all fearing the worst," says Darcy. "He'd promised us a fair dinkum flogging," says Lindner. When Blight breezed into the room, his mood was light. "Okay that's done," he said. "Now a couple of you blokes here have just bought a hotel. We better go down and christen it with a few beers."

Lindner and Flanigan were the new pub owners to whom Blight referred, and the Valley Inn Hotel was only 400 metres from Kardinia Park. "If you want to drink you can drink," Blight instructed. "If you don't want to drink, you don't have to drink ... but you've got to be there for at least two hours."

"And that was our training session!" Lindner laughs. "Darren and I looked at each other and thought *shit, we haven't got enough staff on*."

"Malcolm put $100 on the bar," says Flanigan. "The boys stayed around until quite late that night ... He was really strong on camaraderie outside of the game. An advocate of blokes having a good time."

"With that decision, he changed the whole attitude and persona of the group," says Darcy. "He was an empowering personality and an empowering coach."

Blight strongly believes that Monday is the most important day of the week in a footy club. 'Winning begins Monday' is one of his mottos. "Mondays is when you keep it on track if you've won or get it back on track if you've lost. Mondays were special at Geelong. We'd have a theme every Monday night—just something so it wasn't the same old bloody humdrum every minute."

Blight rattles off some of the Monday refreshers he plotted for the end of training: "We might play Twister, or have a joke night, or a slide night. Or someone to come in for an adding or subtracting test, or a dictionary test … pin the tail on the donkey—camaraderie stuff. You could be harsh on the Saturday or Sunday, and then Monday was the day you'd win them back."

"He kept you on your toes," Lindner says. "You never quite knew where you stood, and that added excitement and variation to the whole equation."

Andrew 'Buck' Rogers played 16 games for the Cats in 1989 and had also played under Blight at Woodville. He made his teammates laugh with this memorable observation: "He's called the wonder coach for a reason, because you wonder what he's going to do next."

11

YOU'LL KEEP

The round six game between Hawthorn and Geelong on 6 May 1989, stands now as a prelude to the larger story to come, and what Blight would refer to as "a forerunner". But it's more than that, too. It's in the ring as a heavyweight contender for best home and away game of all time. For one, it boasts the fifth highest total points (334) in a game. Geelong booted 17 goals in the first half, Hawthorn 17 in the second. It remains the narrowest winning margin (eight points) of any others in the League's ten highest scoring games. Gavin Exell, who wouldn't even make Geelong's best team in September, kicked nine goals in a performance that won him three Brownlow Medal votes. Brereton booted five, as did Buckenara. Yeates kicked three. He also kicked a behind—a miss from ten metres out in the dying seconds, costly as it would have given the Cats one last chance to snatch victory. But as Yeates says in his laconic, Mount Gambier farm boy drawl: "It's pretty hard to swing your leg around a swollen testicle."

Brereton's hit on Yeates at the beginning of the last quarter is a thing of horror. Yeates is competing with Hawks ruckman Greg Dear at a boundary throw-in. The commentators mention that, off screen, Brereton has just been bowled over as the ball went over the line, thanks to a vigorous Ablett shepherd. No free kick is paid. There's a close-up on an incredulous and angry Brereton. The ball spins into play. Dear and Yeates lock arms, eyes on the ball. Brereton comes roaring in from the boundary side, full speed, third man up. He doesn't turn his body when he gets to Yeates, just collects him straight up the middle with his leading knee. Brereton also taps the ball, which adds a scintilla of legitimacy to what is a premeditatedly violent hit. Yeates collapses to the ground. The umpire doesn't award a free kick. Says Peter McKenna in the commentary box: "How could the umpires miss that, Bernie (Quinlan)? That was a dead set charge!"

"I was very frustrated," admits Brereton. "I thought that the umpire had missed a free kick that was blatant. I argued with him ... I'm still to this day staggered that he missed the free kick, and I thought there was a personality component to it—as in 'Cop that, Dermott, you're loud and you're this and that'—and that's when I used to get a little upset."

As Yeates departed the field with that ruptured testicle ("I've still got a lump," he says), Brereton escorted him, letting fly with a few choice sledges. "I just walked alongside the stretcher and badmouthed him," Brereton says. "We did stuff like that in those days."

At the end of the game, Brereton approached Yeates with an outstretched hand. Yeates refused to shake it. "You'll keep," was the Geelong player's tight-lipped reply.

Blight estimates that the action would cost Brereton six to eight weeks if assessed by the modern-day Match Review Panel. "He got him good—so good that Yeater missed the state game (on May 29). And Mark is a very proud man, and he loved playing State footy. We all did. So, he was really dirty, and I knew it."

"I do regret not shaking his hand," Yeates says now, "but I was just absolutely ropable ... From that moment until the next time we played, I was hellbent on evening up with him."

The next time Brereton and Yeates faced off would be in the 1989 Grand Final.

12

NOT FAR AWAY

Blight had tried a radical tactic in the round 6 match. For years Hawthorn had been the measuring stick of the competition. "You knew exactly how Hawthorn was going to line up," Blight says. "They didn't need a lot of tricks—they had a great team."

Blight decided to play not just man on man, but same man on same man. In other words, every player was assigned a particular Hawk, and that match-up was to last the whole day. "If your player comes off, you come off with him," he told his players. "If he goes to the forward pocket, you go to the back pocket." Those were the rules of the day, and there were to be no exceptions. The idea was to concentrate on accountability, each man beating the one opponent. "When you think about it, it's a bit silly," says Blight. "But anyway, we've committed to it."

To say it produced immediate results is an understatement. The Cats boot eight goals in the first quarter and nine in the second. There is a 12-minute stretch in the second quarter during which Geelong piles on seven goals. For half a quarter, this great Hawthorn team that crushed the competition in 1988 and played six consecutive Grand

Finals is reduced to witches' hats.

Ablett is playing his 100th game, and it's as if all the ridiculous highlights of the previous 99 are mere sketches in preparation for the masterpiece he is painting now. There are goals from inside the centre square, running bounces, baulks, soaring marks. He's out on a wing, playing on DiPierdomenico, and three minutes into the second quarter Ablett has ten kicks and three goals. As his third sails through, after a mark that might win the car in a dud year for screamers, Bernie Quinlan up in the commentary box urges a move: "There could be a change here soon. I don't think DiPierdomenico can keep up with Ablett."

Jeans obliges. Dipper is banished to the forward pocket. But, following the 'Blight rule', Ablett has to go with him. So, after lighting up the midfield like a comet, he's suddenly out of the play in the back pocket. If you watch the footage on *YouTube*—(highly recommended viewing)—you'll hear that the commentators are bewildered: "Tony Hall has moved onto Ablett, but Ablett is following DiPierdomenico down to the back pocket. And Hocking is on Hall. So, you have the strange situation where four players are all bunched together in Hawthorn's forward pocket." Ablett stays there for most of the second quarter, which slows him down but not Geelong. "It's actually taken Ablett out of the game," says Peter McKenna. "But that's the discipline of the side. He's down there, and he has to accept it."

Dipper remembers his confusion. "Ablett followed me, and Bairstow followed Bucky (Gary Buckenara) to the other pocket and Dunstall is between us, and we're just watching Geelong slaughter us out of the middle, and I said to Gary Ablett, 'What the hell are we doing down here?'"

The lead balloons out to 56 points. Dipper kicks a goal to get it back to 50.

At half-time Hawthorn trails by 49 points. "Yabby was just so composed," Anderson says. Platten remembers being surprised: "We were eight goals down, you'd think he'd come in and cane us, but he was calm and confident and said we can still win the game." Langford remembers feeling the belief. "We were embarrassed. I remember walking in at half-time and saying, 'This is freaking ridiculous. It can't keep going like this. We can turn this around.' We weren't mouthing platitudes. We believed we could come out and fix it."

Brereton says that he'd like to know the stats on Geelong's clean takeaways from centre bounces in the first half. "If there were 20 centre ground stoppages, I reckon they had clean take-away from 16 of them. Their backline was completely untested. We always thought they weren't brilliant in the back end, and sometimes your luck runs out."

Jeans makes two notable moves. The first is to shift Ayres into the midfield. "He berated Ayresy," says Hawks defender Andy Collins, "which he sometimes did with Gary—he knew he'd get a reaction. He said that he'd cost us goals and that he owed us a better second half."

Over many years, 'Ayresy into the guts' was almost a default Jeans move when the Hawks were in trouble. In an era of smaller bodied midfielders, the man they called 'Conan' was a flint hard, musclebound goliath. He was a sure ball handler, a strong mark, a brilliant kick, a canny reader of the play, and something close to an assassin when he tucked in his elbow, dropped a shoulder and decided to assert himself. Jeans famously called Ayres "a great driver in heavy traffic." Peter Schwab remembers that opposition coaches were always trying to drag Ayres up the ground, because of a perceived lack of speed. "This was the biggest mistake you could ever make because you put him *into the heavy traffic*," Schwab says. "Remember, he played on the wing when he won one of his Norm Smith Medals."

Jeans's second move is to bench DiPierdomenico. By now, the coach has clued into Blight's eccentric tactic. If fielding Dipper in the back pocket could drag Geelong's best player out of the action, he asked himself, what would happen if Dipper went off the ground? It is no small thing; this is long before the bench is used for strategic rests and rotations. In 1989, the best 18, if fit, take the field and stay there. Jeans nevertheless decides to buck convention. His Brownlow medallist warms the pine for the entire third quarter. When Platten tears his pectoral muscle away from his shoulder, there are two Brownlow medallists sitting side by side.

In the opposing coach's box, Blight feels the walls of the prison he'd constructed for himself closing in. "I'm up in the box thinking, 'Awwww c'mon! We're flogging 'em! Gary's firing! He's best on ground by an absolute minute!' And the other blokes in the box are warning me. 'C'mon Malcolm, you said that was the rule! You shouldn't break it'." Blight can't resist. He decides to leave Ablett on the ground, out on the wing.

Then he wavers on another match-up. When Ayres moves to the middle, Yeates expects to go with him. After all, that's the rule. Yeates had done well in the first half, kicking two goals on the dual Norm Smith medallist. He is also strong-bodied and quick. He has experience playing for Victoria on a wing. So, Yeates is surprised when he's met in the centre square by the runner: "No Yeatesy, you go to the back flank."

"I was livid," Yeates says. "Ayres carved us up—he was too big for Couchy (Geelong midfielder Paul Couch) and the boys in the middle. He just carved us up. And I stayed at half-back and got kneed in the balls by Mr. Brereton."

Having looked a certain loser at the main break, Hawthorn wins the game, by eight points. The bizarre nature of this barnstorming goal-fest means the Hawks actually get their own lead out to 20 points, before Yeates bravely returns and kicks a goal, gives one away to teammate Michael Schulze, and takes a brilliant mark 15 metres out, on a slight angle, only to hook the seemingly unmissable chance with 50 seconds remaining. With 30 seconds left Yeates sticks his knees into the back of John Kennedy Jnr and pulls down a spectacular mark, 30 metres from goal, but for reasons unknown, a free kick is paid against him and the Hawks hold on.

James Morrissey, Dipper's replacement, has been a star. Buckenara, Dunstall and Brereton all kick three goals in the second half. The sealer comes from Ayres himself, streaming forward from beyond 50, his Conan locks flying. He's brutalised the Geelong midfield, and is clearly the matchwinner. Ablett plays well in the second half, but not to the standard of his sublime first. As the crowd pours onto the ground in the seconds after the siren, players sprint for the race, and the umpires are protected from enraged Geelong fans by two horse-mounted police officers.

"Malcolm broke his own rule that day," is all Tim Darcy says.

"I said after the game that I'd blown it," Blight says. "I don't remember reviewing the game a lot because I figured that if I'd taken Gary off, we probably would have hung on. Who knows—it was one of those things I didn't do very often but I did do that day. I made the rule. I'm a rule-maker on certain things." Blight grins wistfully. "It was just … he was on fire! At half-time, he had *six* votes in the Brownlow!"

With that win, Hawthorn went to 5-1 and strengthened its air of invincibility. Curran, who was in the Seconds that day, remembers it as a turning point. "I wrote about it," he says, referring to his *Sunday Age* column. "Yabby was his old self when we came back to training, talking about the performance being 'real good' and chastising us for being so far down: 'You can't expect to do that every week and get away with it'." The Hawks also knew that if they met Geelong again in 1989, it would be in September. "In some ways we had the psychological edge," says Curran.

Geelong was 3-3, with an enhanced reputation for flakiness—imperious at home and vulnerable elsewhere. But Blight remembers feeling positive. "'They're the best,' I told the players. 'They're coming off premierships, they're the dominant team—and we missed by a kick and a bit. We can learn from that. Let's wait if we can get to them in September. Let's just put that away. We're not far away'."

13

TORRENTIAL

If the round six loss had dented Geelong's confidence, it wasn't immediately obvious over the next five weeks. Having attained the unwelcome record of becoming the first team to kick 25 goals in a League match and still lose, the Cats went on a rampage, winning by 119, 129 and 134 points in their next three games. The following week, against fifth-placed Collingwood, they won by 'only' 11 goals, which was followed by a nine-goal win over the fourth-placed Bombers, kicking 12 goals to four on a mud-caked MCG. After a 69-point win over Melbourne in round 12 (the previously second-placed Demons only kicked 2.8 for the day), the Cats had surged into second place with a percentage of 170—30 per cent better than the Hawks. This was all taking place during the second wettest winter in Victorian history.

Blight says he tweaked a few things on the defensive side after the cavalier losses against Fitzroy and Hawthorn. "As much as I wanted them to freewheel, I'm not stupid," he says. "There are some defensive things you've got to do as well." He made a list of the hard things in football: chasing, tackling, smothering, long punches. Blight shared the list with his players and set a target of 'one hundred hard things' per game. "From that week I think we went on a bit of a run and started winning."

"It was exhilarating," says Darcy. "Our game was predicated on attack and built around our better players. We had good midfielders and we had very, very good forwards."

"It was what I thought football was all about," smiles Lindner, "and the spectators thought that way too. We used to go up on the bus, and I'd sit next to Robert Scott and we'd have a five-dollar wager on how many people would go to the game. We'd run out and there'd be 60,000 people there. In the past we'd played in front of ten or twelve. It was an exciting brand of footy."

Jeans also strove for the right balance between defence and attack. Forty tackles per game was always the target number for the Hawks. "You can all get two tackles a game," he told his men. "That's not too much to ask!" It was drilled into his players relentlessly. In the lead-up to the Grand Final, Jeans would again ask for the magic 40, calling it 'Operation Tackle', a nod to his old policing days.

"We were a high possession team," Brereton says. "We used to honour the lead, we hit short chip-ups all day long ... But we were also a very good high-pressure team. It sounds trite now, but we laid 40 tackles and they're not your 40 tackles from today—40 tackles in that era meant that you had the opposition terrified and under pressure. Because they were real tackles. You didn't have 16 blokes all standing around a pack and endless stoppages where you pick up easy tackles ... if you could lay a tackle back then, you got paid holding the ball."

The Hawks didn't always get to the 40—in one representative six-week spell they had 13, 37, 42, 35, 17 and 29—but it remained something of an obsession for Jeans. And if they ever did get there, he was a happy coach.

After 'the streak', Geelong's scoring rate reduced from torrential to a steady shower. They lost two in a row, to Melbourne and Collingwood, in rounds 16 and 17, and another to West Coast in Perth in round 20.

Otherwise they consistently did enough to win, and to win with flair.

Hawthorn also dropped one game to Melbourne in mid-season and had a surprise loss to the lowly Brisbane Bears in a low-scoring game at Carrara in round 20. But that was it. The super consistent Hawks finished top of the ladder on 19-3, two games clear of Essendon, and the Cats were a game further back in third, on sixteen wins. Under the old McIntyre final five system, Hawthorn had the week off in the first week of the finals. Essendon would play Geelong in the qualifying final at the MCG.

It was Geelong's first finals series since 1981. Sleepy Hollow was well and truly awake.

14

ANGRY YOUNG MEN

It seemed like a good idea at the time. In fact, it doesn't seem like such a bad idea even now. On the day of Geelong's first final against Essendon, Blight organised for the team bus to leave a little earlier, allowing time for a surprise stop. "Because no-one had played in the finals for a long time, I wanted to take them back to their childhoods," Blight says. "I wanted them to play kick-to-kick in the park."

He chose "some ground in Footscray just off the West Gate freeway" to reconnect his men with their nascent love for the game. As the Geelong players tumbled out of the bus, Blight gave a short speech, which he remembers going something like: "Most of you grew up on one of these little suburban grounds. Let's just have a kick, and then let's take that with us to the MCG!"

Lindner remembers the speech: "He goes, 'This is where you all come from, where it all started, and now you have the opportunity to reach the peak of football. But remember where your roots were!'"

Very quickly, the players remembered where their *boots* were. "We're running around there in our Hush Puppies and slipping all over the joint, and fumbling the ball," says Yeates. Says Flanigan: "The park might have looked okay from the top of the Westgate but it was actually a cow paddock, and the wind was blowing 80 miles an hour."

"We must have been in a wind tunnel," agrees Blight. "It's blowing 90 miles an hour and I just thought, oh god … It's one of those calls you make. Blokes could hardly hit the ball with their foot—it was blowing out of their hands! I gave it 10-15 minutes thinking the whole time, 'Oh what did I do this for?'"

"Any shred of confidence we had going into the game was destroyed in about 10 minutes of kick-to-kick under the Westgate," laughs Flanigan. Essendon booted 24 goals to 11 and won the right to play Hawthorn in the second semi-final. Geelong would face a sudden death first semi- final against Melbourne, the previous year's losing Grand Finalist.

Blight apologised to his team immediately after the Essendon game, admitting that the change to the pre-game routine had backfired. Speaking to Mike Sheahan on Fox Footy's *Open Mike*, the late Paul Couch said, "That was the great thing about Blighty. If he did something wrong, he apologised for it … I respect him highly and I always have."

Yeates believes the turnaround began on the bus trip back to Geelong. Blight was Melbourne-based, so usually drove to and from games with wife Patsy. But after the defeat, Blight decided to take the return trip with his team. "What do you blokes normally do?" Blight asked Damian Drum, who'd just played his first senior game for the year and was close to the coach both in age (29) and relationship. "Well, sometimes we put ice in a plastic bin and fill it up with cans," Drum replied, "and then maybe stop to fill it up again at Werribee."

Earlier in the year, Blight had applied a handbrake to the scale of drinking on the bus trips back to Geelong. Says Drum, "At the start of '89, Malcolm said that it was unprofessional and that we had to look after ourselves better." But on this night, Blight waived these restrictions and detoured to a pub in North Melbourne. The plastic bin was stocked.

"We all started talking positively," remembers Yeates. "We talked about the Hush Puppies and how we wouldn't be doing that again. And I reckon that was a really good night, a rebuilding night. We licked our wounds and we got ourselves back on track."

"He was very bullish about our chances the following week," Drum remembers. "His whole persona was built around positivity."

It was during the bus trip that the coach called over his two most prolific ball winners, Couch and Bairstow. They were both stars of the competition, running first and second in the VFL for number of disposals (both averaged 26.9 a game), and 50 possessions clear of the third place-getter. Blight had prepared a bombshell for his key on-ballers. "OK, against Melbourne next week, you two boys will be starting on the bench."

Says Blight: 'In those days, the bench meant the bench. There were no rotations." He remembers Bairstow and Couch not taking the news particularly well, "but I was pretty positive, pretty stern that that was going to happen."

Couch and Bairstow, like many of their teammates, had struggled in that first final. But Blight's decision was based on their next opponent, the John Northey-coached Melbourne. In their previous two clashes—a pre-season night fixture, and Geelong's round 16 loss—Northey had tagged the star duo to good effect. "That was one of my rules," Blight says. "If something hasn't worked once, and then twice, you don't just do the same thing over and over. I'd already thought about it straight after the game, that they were going to be on the bench. It was probably tough on them. Oh well, I got dragged in a Grand Final too."

Blight also ignored accepted convention and put his players in the firing line at training that week. He asked his football manager, Gary Fletcher, to source a set of Melbourne jumpers. Fletcher found a local team in Geelong that wore the red and blue. "A bit scungy but good enough," remembers Blight. He then set his men upon one another in full contact competitive work.

"Half had Melbourne jumpers on, half had Geelong," remembers Darcy. "You had to do things to the blokes in the Melbourne jumpers. It's probably the one time in my life I could've said to you, hand on heart, that there's no way we're going to lose next week ... The way he prepared us ... There was a level of fierceness."

"Apparently it was the hardest session ever seen at the Geelong football club—ever," grins Blight. "That's what everyone said. And yet, it (the competitive drill) went for seven minutes. I know because I've still got notes of every training session I ever had."

The following Sunday, Geelong went out and thrashed the Demons by ten goals. Ablett kicked 7.7 from 24 disposals, and Blight was good to his word, starting Couch and Bairstow on the bench. In just his second game for the year, Drum was parachuted into one of the team's vacant midfield roles. "At quarter-time we were up by ten points in a really hard-fought game,' says Drum, "And Malcolm was buoyant, saying, 'We've got these blokes, and look what we've got waiting on the bench! Look what we've got waiting in reserve!'"

Says Blight, "When they came on, they had 20-plus (disposals) each in virtually a half of football. They were angry young men, which you know, set us on the way to a Grand Final."

15

DEMOLITION DERMOTT

Hawthorn's second semi-final win against Essendon is remembered largely for 20 minutes of physical destruction inflicted by Dermott Brereton. Brereton went goalless that day, and had a modest statistical tally of 14 disposals, but for a period in the second quarter, he brutalised the opposition. Says Brereton: "That second quarter against Essendon was the one time in over 200 games of League footy where I swung a game without touching the footy."

The first act of aggression was aimed at Platten's tagger, Darren 'Daisy' Williams. It was a full torso bear-hug tackle, emphatic and not particularly dirty, and indeed Brereton wins a free kick for holding the ball. The reverse angle shows his arms slipping high, which may or may not have done the damage, and may or may not have been deliberate. Injured, Williams leaves the ground and doesn't resume his tagging duties. Platten goes from one kick in a meagre first quarter to 23 for the game, and the consensus among media pundits is that he's the best on ground.

Platten says he could always call on Brereton for help when the taggers were getting to him. "Dermott was always there," Platten says. "He knew I'd get tagged and thumped around, and he always said, 'Rat, if you're ever in trouble, just bring him down my end and I'll see what I can do for you.' That's the relationship I had with him."

"I thought Johnny Platten was our most important player," says Brereton. "They used to push it to the letter of the law giving it to Johnny Platten. The rules permitted that if the opposition player was within five metres of the ball, I could run in and bump them, down the centre, to the head, and as long as it wasn't an elbow, I could bump them out of the game. I thought that was a loophole in the rules. Even back in the day I'm quoted as saying that it's not the right way to play football. But it was part of the rules and so I took advantage of it."

The second of the Brereton hits that day is one of the most famous in football history—a sweetly timed hip and shoulder which knocks Paul Vander Haar into unconsciousness. It's impossible to watch it without wincing. The action takes place near the boundary line, on the members' side, so the camera is close. Vander Haar is paddling the ball along the ground, struggling to pick it up, a wily veteran suddenly as vulnerable as a schoolboy. Brereton approaches from ninety degrees at full pace, elbow tucked in, eyes on his mark, who can't see him coming. He doesn't jump in the air, which would make it an illegal charge, and the ball is within ten metres, which is the allowable perimeter for a hip and shoulder. It's a moment of pure, unmitigated violence, but as Brereton explains, perfectly legal and perfectly executed in the context of the era. The result is serious concussion for Vander Haar. but the umpire doesn't even award him a free kick. In fact, on-baller Darrin Pritchard picks up the spilled ball and runs into an open goal. In the absence of Vander Haar, Terry Daniher is moved to the backline and the Bombers lose potency up forward.

Next, Brereton is slung in a tackle by Tim Watson, and to the great fortune of Watson, Brereton and football folklore, the wild haymaker that Brereton throws at his opponent slides over Watson's head by a matter of centimetres.

Finally, it's Andrew Manning's turn. Perhaps sensing vulnerability, Manning has been playing a very physical game on Hawthorn's 20-game rookie, Dean Anderson. Manning, the former Saint, playing only his second game for the Bombers, has featured in only six wins in five years of League football, and now he looks like he's taking out half a decade of frustration on his 22-year-old opponent. "He basically wanted to intimidate me," Anderson says. "I was playing half-forward, and Manning came up to me and gave me some profanities and stood on my feet and whacked me a few times."

When the opportunity presented itself, Brereton fixed up Manning as well. After the game, considering Brereton's demolition job, Bombers coach Kevin Sheedy is more envious than bitter: "We could do with that sort of player in our side."

Says Brereton: "In this day and age, I'd be looking at 15 weeks for those three, but in those days, it was deemed good, hard footy."

I ask Dermott about the morality of it all. He's thoughtful with his answer, as he is at most times. "The morality of it isn't great," he says. "Because you're actually hurting somebody. Not that I spent all week going, 'I'm going to target somebody.' It never really happened that way. I'd go out there thinking *football, football, football*. Then, for half a moment, I'd recognise that some player is open, and then go at him and try to take him out of the game."

After leading by only four points at half time, Hawthorn wins the second semi by a comfortable 36 points. While Brereton bludgeons, Curran kicks two important goals and accidentally breaks Paul Hamilton's nose with his forehead in a front-on tackle. Dunstall kicks six. Buckenara, three. A turning point comes when Dipper runs down Tony Antrobus, gripping him by the shorts and dragging him to ground like a lion seizing a gazelle—one of his seven tackles on the day.

Hawthorn lays 50 tackles, Essendon just 20. Hawthorn had barged its way into a seventh consecutive Grand Final like the school bully stomping through the tuck-shop line. Not only was Hawthorn the best performed team in the competition—it had lost only six games in two years—it was the toughest and most intimidating.

Whoever played Hawthorn on Grand Final day would need to be ready.

16

TRIBUNAL NIGHT

Brereton wasn't the only Hawk to hit Andrew Manning in the second semi-final. Peter Schwab did too, a forearm to the back of the head in a marking contest that earned him a date with the VFL Tribunal. Schwab was 28-years-old and hadn't been suspended in 157 games, which included Hawthorn's 1983, 1986 and 1988 premierships. "I just put the forearm into the back of the head," admits Schwab. "I was frustrated because I was having a reasonably hard day on Michael Long, who could play a bit. He was quick and slippery, and I'm thinking to myself, 'The way I'm going, if we win …' Well, you start worrying about your spot for next week."

It was a busy Monday at the Tribunal. Garry Hocking was fined for tripping Peter Rohde but was free to play in the preliminary final. Mark Yeates and Melbourne's Tony Campbell were reported for striking one another. Campbell was cleared. Yeates received a one-match suspension for his retaliatory punch. Unlike Schwab, he had the cushion of a preliminary final. "I was lucky to get one week," Yeates admits. "Thank heavens I only got one week."

Schwab wasn't so lucky. He tried to paint it as a clumsy spoil but the Tribunal waved off the excuses and gave him a three-match suspension. "In the context of the era, it (the hit) wasn't that bad," says Schwab, with the heaviness that goes with missing out on a sporting contest that will live on in the history books. "I may have been better suited by today's environment of match review," Schwab says. After coaching the Hawks between 2000 and 2004, he became chairman of the Match Review Committee in 2005, so maybe he has some insight? He chuckles: "Although no, I still probably would have got rubbed out."

Schwab was an absolute favourite of his coach. "Every week Yab gave Peter Schwab a job," Brereton explains. "Jeansy would say, 'Son, I have a job for you. I want you to play on Wayne Johnston, I want you to play on Gavin Brown. Today you've got a bloke called Daicos.' Never once did Schwabby say, 'I don't want to do that.' Jeans loved Peter Schwab for his dedication to the team and its fortunes."

For Schwab, the love was reciprocal, but he remembers his coach's knack for robust feedback, his ability to be "cutting and funny at the same time". Before the second semi-final in 1983, a young Schwab stood at the top of the MCG race, psyching himself up, thinking he was one win away from playing in his first Grand Final. "Yab calls me over, and I think, 'Oh, he's gonna give me a last-minute word of wisdom,' and he looks at me and he goes, 'Listen, get it into your head, you're not a real good player'."

Brereton remembers similar comments being directed at DiPierdomenico. "Dipper won the Brownlow (in 1986) and then for the first half a dozen games of the next year he drifted away from what made him a Brownlow medallist," Brereton says. Instead of being a bulldozing wingman who could break the first tackle and hit up a target, according to Brereton, Brownlow Dipper was suddenly trying blind turns, baulks, and party tricks, and was getting caught holding the ball four or five times each week. Says Brereton: "At half-time of game five or game six, Yabby looked at him and said, 'Dipper, what am I going to do with yer, son?' Dipper kept looking up, trying to hold the stare. Then Yabby said, 'Robert, you're a very good player, when you don't think you are!'"

Chris Wittman's favourite along these lines was when Jeans would say: "When I stop yelling at yer son, you'll know I've given up on yer!"

Dipper remembers Jeans being obsessed with the ever-improving fleet of vehicles in the carpark at Glenferrie Oval. "I hope yers are not getting ahead of yerselves? You know when I first came to this club, I looked in the bloody car park and there were bloody Holdens and Fords! Now there are BMWs and Ferraris!"

One anecdote that John Kennedy Jnr shared in his Jeans eulogy was the difference between his coach's quiet public face—his staunch defence of his players—and what he said behind closed doors. "After a bad loss, his piercing blue eyes would scan the room, and he'd say phrases such as, 'Blokes on ego trips and lairising,' and, 'If the cap fits, wear it!' ... and 'Don't worry about me, I go out there and defend ya to the press, I'll make something up for you. You just make sure you have fun tonight! Don't let that performance get in the way of ya dancing—oh we can't have that! Off ya go! Hope ya bloody beer tastes sour!'"

Dipper says Jeans would sit in the sauna on Sundays, listening but rarely speaking, and store up stories as ammunition. "Son, yer've got to attack the ball with more ferocity! Maybe you're still day dreamin' about Cynthia from the bloody Tunnel!" (The Tunnel being the nightclub of choice for footballers in those years.)

When you speak to them now, all the players try on a Jeans impression. His was such a distinctive voice—the squeezed, elongated vowels, a clipped baritone that almost belongs to broadcasts of the Movietone era. Schwab's is as good as any. "I remember he called me up one Friday. 'I've got a job for you, son. I don't think you can do it ... I need you to play on Wayne Schimmelbusch. He's a real good player, you're not that good. I don't care if you don't get a kick as long as he doesn't get a kick'." The game was played, North won, and Schimmelbusch kicked three goals and had 30 possessions. "Yabby comes up to me after the game and says, 'Son, you couldn't do the job'. And I say, 'Well, you said it would be hard.' And he says, 'I didn't think it would be *that* hard,' and I thought I'd be a bit smart, so I said, 'Yab, I kept one end of the bargain up ... you said it didn't matter if *I* didn't get a kick.' And he just smiles and says, 'Yes, yes. Well, I dunno how you'll go this week'."

For Peter Schwab, after the second semi-final of 1989, there would be no next week. And for one lucky player on the fringe of selection, suddenly a golden ticket was on offer.

17

WHERE'S LANGERS?

In 1989 footballers had not only training and playing to contend with, but day jobs.

At Geelong, even coach Blight still clocked on for his management job. Couch and Garry Hocking worked as garbos, regularly running a ten-kilometre route on concrete, heaving bags over their shoulders, the Friday morning before a Saturday game. Lindner and Flanigan owned the pub. "We had the second largest beer turnover in country Victoria that year," Flanigan says. Andrew Bews was a plumber, as were Tuck and Kennedy over at Hawthorn. Future AFL Football Operations Manager Steve Hocking was a bricklayer. Gary Ablett drove trucks for Geelong President Ron Hovey. Mark Bairstow was a thoroughbred horse trainer. Says Flanigan: "He was always pretty stingy sharing tips." Mark Yeates drove a backhoe and remembers, in Grand Final week, getting out of the digger to "have a chat" with some men laying pipes, who happened to be expressing "a loud and negative opinion" about his teammates. "They didn't have a clue who was sitting on the backhoe," Yeates says. "I just hopped off and said, 'Listen you guys, shut the fuck up. It's not right what you're saying.' I had a can with them and went to training the next day."

Over at Hawthorn, Platten owned the Prince Alfred Hotel near Melbourne University. Schwab, Curran and Collins were teachers. Mew was a builder, Buckenara a salesman. Defender Scott Maginness was studying to become a chiropractor and spent 1989 turning up to lectures wearing the badges of League football. "I had a broken nose twice that year," he says. "You'd come into lectures with black eyes, and in the pre-season my jaw was broken, and I lost teeth."

Dermott Brereton wore several hats, but most of them involved, well, just *being Dermott*. He did paid appearances at clubs and hotels. He was what modern-day marketers would call a 'brand ambassador', spruiking everything from footy boots to *Tip Top* bread. He did marketing jobs at Hawthorn, ran a string of fashion boutiques, and even worked at the VFL for two years between 1982 and 1984. On one occasion, he borrowed League Media Manager Ian McDonald's car to run an errand. When he returned it, he dropped the keys on the older man's desk. "There you go Macca. Your car's a write-off." Brereton had opened the driver side door into traffic and a passing vehicle ripped it from its hinges. Another time he punched on with a truckie who'd taken offence at his two-finger salute. But he was always Dermie—thanks to the cheeky grin, the eye-catching blond locks and the chutzpah to charm his way out of trouble, nobody stayed mad at him for long. Profiling Brereton, journalist Gary Linnell spoke to one of the Hawk's co-workers in the VFL House era: "Everybody got on well with him … I don't think he applied himself very hard… but he had a good personality." In the end it was Brereton who chose to leave. "He was making more money than [then VFL boss] Jack Hamilton anyway."

Chris Langford worked in the white-collar world of property development. His employer was Lend Lease, and every morning the Hawks' full-back started early in order to leave early and make training. It was a harrowing workload, and he often struggled to arrive on time. Dean Anderson, then an accounting graduate, also worked in the city, and would also sometimes be late. "I'd be running in, a bit frazzled," says Anderson, "and I'd pass Langers who would just be waltzing in, cool and casual."

Langford was unflappable on and off the field. Whereas some teammates had hotted-up Monaros or Peter Brock Special Commodores, Langford rode a Triumph motorcycle, regal and green. As Anderson says, "Langers is right out there as a fully professional, articulate, beautiful man, and then he rides this beautiful bike to training. And after training he goes to ride home and it's fully dismantled." To this day, John Kennedy remains a strong suspect.

All this is to say that in September 1989, Langford was tired, and relishing Hawthorn's non-involvement in week three of the finals. "I was excited about the footy, but my mind and body were more than ready for a rest," he says, "so having a week off was great timing from my point of view."

But it was only a week off *playing*. Training continued, and Jeans scheduled an extra session for Saturday morning. Attendance was of course compulsory, but afterwards, Langford planned to drive to his brother's place at Euroa for a relaxing weekend. At the end of training, Jeans threw a bomb under his plans. "Right, get your tickets off Hooky (Hawthorn Football Manger, John Hook)," the coach said. "We'll all meet out at Waverley at 2pm. We're going to watch Geelong and Essendon together."

"Nobody had mentioned this before," says Langford. "I'm thinking, 'What the hell, I don't want to wait till 5.30 to drive up the highway. I'll just watch it on TV'." And that's exactly what he did. Langford didn't attend the preliminary final with the rest of his teammates. He wasn't there to see Geelong thump the Bombers by 15 goals—a 170-point turnaround on the qualifying final result. Most importantly of all, he wasn't there to see Gary Ablett play football as well as football had ever been played. 22 kicks, 10 marks, 8 goals and 5 behinds. Pure sporting perfection.

As Ablett's outrageous feats unfolded, Jeans summoned his best defender. "Get Langers," he said. "I want to show him what to look out for with Ablett."

The awkward news had to be broken to him. 'Sorry Yab. Langers hasn't shown up. We're not sure where he is.'

This was all before mobile phones, the pre-email era. When Langford got back to his answering machine on Sunday night, the message count was high, and he knew the shit had hit the fan. John Hook rang later that night: "Where were you? Yab's not happy, he'll speak to you tomorrow."

18

UP ALL NIGHT

In the euphoria of the Waverley rooms, Blight congratulated his players and issued a simple instruction: "Enjoy the weekend, and we'll have a chat Monday."

History has recorded that his players did enjoy themselves that weekend. There is no more infamous commute in football history than the one Bill Brownless and Barry Stoneham made from Zulu nightclub in Geelong to their homes, at 5am on Sunday morning, clinging to the side of a garbage truck. The driver didn't require directions. He knew where they lived. Peter Dickson, footy documentarian and brother of 1989 Hawk, the late Robert Dickson, made a funny little animation of the trip for his wonderful film, *1989, The Final Story*. Said Brownless to Dickson: "We all got swept up in it … we probably didn't prepare as well as we should have, a couple of us." Brownless also said something similar to *The Geelong Advertiser*: "We had a few beers, after the prelim final. We had a good drink, like we'd made it I suppose. We trained all that week, but knowing the Hawthorn side, they would have been in bed ready to go."

Tim Darcy's old side, St Joseph's, had won a Grand Final in the local League. "There was no way I wasn't going out with my mates," he told James Button. "I stayed out too late and woke feeling sick and dehydrated the next day. I didn't know any better. Malcolm didn't read us the riot act."

As Couch told Mike Sheahan on *Open Mike*: "We really didn't know what we were doing ... when we won the preliminary final we went out, had a few drinks enjoyed each other's company, and we just went out to play in '89." Couch said the same to Jenny McCasey of the *Herald Sun* in 2007: "We were just kids who had a crazy month, enjoying ourselves."

In the pain of the eventual one-kick loss, the cataloguing of these preliminary final weekend transgressions is mostly self-flagellation by Geelong players. Over the 30 years since, such tales have been spun into a well-worn trope: a week away from the biggest game of their lives, the Cats spiralled into a long night of bacchanalian excess, while the Hawks did everything that diligent, responsible reigning premiers are meant to do. Yoga at dawn and eight solid hours! Ayres has been quoted as saying that Jeans checked in with players with a phone call every night that week. I called Ayres seeking confirmation on this. He laughed his loud, deep laugh. "That story might have had a bit of mayo on it," he says. "Allan was very much about personal responsibility. He would have told us what he expected, and to look after ourselves, but in the end, it would have been up to the individual to make his own decision."

So, let it be said: the Hawks weren't in bed at 9pm.

Indeed, Hawthorn players were out on that Saturday, too. Nineteen-year-old Greg Madigan was in the senior training group but considered himself long odds to be a Grand Final starter after playing just five games in his debut season, the last of them in round 20. He put his drink card where his mouth was, by going to the notorious Chasers nightclub with his teenaged mates, as he did most weeks. "I remember waiting in line, and Dermott came out of the nightclub to go home,"

Madigan says. "I don't know what time it was, but he turned around and got us in." So that's two who were out. It sounds like Dermott got an early night *within the context of being at Chasers*. Brereton says that although he and his snakeskin cowboy boots were a familiar sight in the nightclubs of Melbourne, he only allowed himself an alcoholic drink three times a year during football season. Anderson confesses that, "if Dermott was at Chasers, I was probably there too. We used to go out together a lot. He was like an older brother."

Blight has no regrets about encouraging his players to savour the moment and to have a good time. "Football is hard work. But if you don't enjoy the good times, I don't know what you're doing it for. And the whole idea is to win, and when you win, you don't want blokes getting rolling drunk and all that, but if you don't feel good about yourself when you win … what the hell are you doing it for? So, I never put them in nappies and sent them home to bed. I mean for goodness sake enjoy yourselves, enjoy the company of your teammates and your wives or girlfriends. It never bothered me."

So yes, Geelong may have partied harder. Theirs was a younger list with more unmarried men, and they'd just won a preliminary final by 94 points. But neither Hawthorn nor Geelong micromanaged its players' social lives. Drinking after a game was not taboo, even drinking to excess, and for VFL footballers of 1989 a big Saturday night was nothing new. And players from both clubs followed well-worn patterns that were part of the rhythms of their week. For Michael Tuck, that might have meant stopping at the bottle shop on Glenferrie Road and sipping a few stubbies on the way home to Berwick. For the younger players, it meant nightclubs. You played, you socialised, and then you recovered on all fronts, and the focus shifted to training well for the next game. Although sports science now says there's a better way, it's unfair to say that Geelong's 1989 preliminary final celebrations had a decisive influence on events a week later.

I agree with Blight—the Cats didn't lose it on the dance floor at Zulus.

19

THE BIGGEST JOB

On the Monday afternoon of Grand Final week Chris Langford received his spray. "It was entirely justified," he says.

Of all the Jeans testimonials I heard while researching this book, Langford's is the most restrained, the least hagiographic. "He was the coach. I was the young player ... he was always the senior figure, he was older, cut from a different cloth. It was a bit like being a student at school. He was the teacher ... I didn't go to school expecting to be best mates with my teachers. I didn't go to footy expecting to be best mates with the coach."

Five years earlier, in 1984, Langford was on the receiving end of one of the toughest of Grand Final selection blows. It's a famous Hawthorn story. On the Tuesday or Wednesday, Jeans asked ruckman Ian 'General' Paton if he wanted to play in a Grand Final. His reply: "I'd eat shit to play in a Grand Final." Thankfully such drastic action wasn't required, but Jeans told Paton he'd play and swore him to secrecy. Paton's parents rang from Tasmania during the week and asked if he'd be playing. "I'm not in the team," he replied. The first they knew to the contrary was watching the game on television, seeing their son run through the banner.

Paton was included at the expense of a young Langford, who was 21-years-old, and had played 22 games for the year. He'd played a bit on the wing, a bit as second ruckman to Michael Byrne or Paton. He was not yet the chiselled, Hall of Fame defender he would become but, after being on the outer at the end of his debut season of 1983, he was now a senior team regular, and had played every game since round eight. On the Thursday night he was named in the Grand Final line-up. On the Friday night, at 7.30pm, having attended team meetings and the Grand Final parade, he received the devastating phone call. "I'm worried about their talls," said Jeans. "We need another ruckman. I'm putting in Paton, sorry, you're out." Then there's the part that seems to still hurt Langford. Jeans instructed him to act as if he was playing. "Bring your bag. Wear your gear. Sheedy will have his spies there … Don't tell your family."

"So, a lot of paranoia," says Langford. "In terms of rubbing your nose in it, making you rock up and not tell anyone, that was pretty stupid." Hawthorn led by 23 points at three-quarter time but lost that Grand Final, overrun by the fast finishing Bombers by 24 points. The Jeans-Langford relationship repaired itself, and Langford became one of the great defenders of all time, but the two never bonded in the same way as Jeans did with other players. "I could look around the room … a lot of the guys who were the same age or younger would crack jokes, have that love, and have a great relationship with him. It wasn't like I didn't see it, it's just that wasn't me, I didn't have that chemistry … It's not that I held grudges … I loved him, I thought he was great … I just didn't want to hug him and high five him, you know?"

In 1989 there was never any risk that Langford's Euroa transgression would cost him his place in the team. Geelong's forward line, boasting Stoneham, Brownless and Ablett, had helped Geelong score more total points (2916) than any other team in the history of the game.

Langford, alongside Mew, was a senior figure charged with stopping the onslaught. His punishment for not watching the preliminary final with his teammates was never going to be more than a reprimand.

At the team meeting, on the Friday, Scott Maginness received the news that he'd be playing on Ablett. "They said I'd done a good job on Garry Lyon in the '88 Grand Final, and they wanted me to do that again, and perhaps use Langers to be more offensive, to give more drive. And that was basically the extent of it. There was no 'how you should play him and what you should do.' Yab just said, 'You're playing on him—stop him,' and that was it."

It'd been a race against time for Maginness to make the team. He'd played every game for the year, and was an automatic selection if fit, but rolled his ankle in the second quarter of the second semi-final and missed the second half. He couldn't have played preliminary final week ("No way, it was still up like a balloon") but by the Tuesday of Grand Final week, the swelling had reduced. By the Thursday, Maginness was a lock for the team. And by the Thursday night, he had the job of all jobs.

Gary Ablett, the man who'd kicked 15 goals in two weeks.

Gary Ablett, the man some were already calling the best to pull on a pair of boots.

Gary Ablett, the man in the most scintillating form of his life.

After the meeting, Brereton came up to Maginness and said, "Mate that's a really good challenge. If you stop him you could win the Norm Smith!" Maginness laughs. "I'm thinking *I just got in the team!* I just got in the team and Dermott's saying to me, 'All you have to do is beat him and you win the Norm Smith'."

Langford was surprised and disappointed he didn't get the Ablett job. He approached Jeans after the meeting and asked why he hadn't. "Yab said, 'Because you didn't come to the game at Waverley on Saturday. I wanted to talk to you and show you and highlight certain things about the way he was playing, and what you need to do, and you weren't there, so Scotty Maginness is playing on him'."

Did he really change his mind? Andy Collins doubts Jeans would deviate from what he regarded as his optimal lineup. But he also says that Jeans knew Langford was his best one-on-one defender. "As a coach now [Collins coaches Williamstown in the VFL], I can kind of sympathise. Yab might not have wanted to start with his best option, because if it's 15 minutes into the first quarter of a Grand Final, and Ablett's kicked three, where do you go from there? Your Plan A hasn't worked and that's not a good feeling. So maybe Yab started with his Plan B, hoping it would work, because it would be a huge benefit for the team if it came off. But if it didn't, he still had Langers in his back pocket, his prime asset. And that's how it turned out." Langford says that Jeans would constantly challenge him—"He'd needle me to get a reaction, to test me. It was all a test."

Looking back on events of those times, I think it's most likely Jeans gave Maginness the job on Ablett for the reasons he stated to the team—that he thought he could keep him to a few goals, and he wanted Langford released to a more attacking role. But passing Langford after the meeting, he might not have been able to resist a little verbal jab, a motivational barb, an overhang from the reprimand on the Monday. The alternative is that he told Langford the truth, that he did change his mind on who should get the job, and that the Euroa trip played a part. Jeans isn't around to tell us.

In any event, the job went to Maginness. He drove home determined not to be overawed. "Things go through your mind," he says. "You're wanting to not make a fool of yourself. You're wanting to contribute and play your role. You're wanting to beat your man. You're wanting to be attacking and you're wanting to be brave. You want to be all those things that you know you've always dreamed about. But knowing at any point it could all go horribly pear-shaped."

When he returned to the Maginness family home, he told his brothers the good news.

"Oh shit," was their succinct reply.

20

A BROWNLOW PREMONITION

After the wettest of winters, the sun shone on Melbourne and Geelong in the last week of September 1989. In the city of Geelong, there was sheer fandemonium. "Every second house had blue and white out the front," remembers Blight. "Every factory, every business. The training sessions, they were enormous. It was just amazing. Amazing." Blight took the 1963 premiership Cup to a dinner hosted by the Board. "This is what we're playing for," he said. "It's pretty special."

"My attitude was: 'Let's not hide it, we're actually playing in a Grand Final. You don't want to downplay it or overplay it. You just play it'," he says. His side was to play in Geelong's first Grand Final since its 1967 loss to Richmond.

Flanigan remembers running through a banner to get onto the ground to train. "That was a bit weird," he grins. "It was almost a ticketed event to attend training. There were 20,000 people in the grandstand." Flanigan says he didn't get carried away. "It was very festive, blue and white streamers in all the shopfronts, all that, but working in the pub from eight in the morning to ten or eleven at night, five or six days a week, you didn't really get out in the community to see it. The town was abuzz. But we had a job to do and didn't get overly fussed."

As if the Kardinia wildfire of hope and happiness needed any further stoking, Paul Couch won the Brownlow Medal on the Monday night with 22 votes. Platten was runner-up, two votes back. The boy from Boggy Creek had a stellar year, leading the competition for total disposals. He was a terrific ball user, had a neat sidestep, could hit targets left and right, and ran as hard as anyone in the competition. Everyone in Geelong and the wider football world loved that he worked as a garbo for the local council. Before he died unexpectedly in 2016 at just 51 years of age, Couch told Mike Sheahan that running the bins "was really good for freeing up your body" after the hard work of games and training. "I'd think, 'If I can run eight to ten kilometres on a Friday, how are they going to stop you on Saturday?'"

His win was also another marker of the Blight ascension. In the back half of 1988, Couch had played four games in the reserves. The demotion was a disciplinary action. In a team meeting, Devine had put it to the players that there were some who didn't want him as coach. Devine then asked the playing group to speak up: "Who doesn't want me here?" Couch recounted it to Sheahan with that cheeky grin footy fans fell in love with on Brownlow night: "My dad always told me to tell the truth." So, he did: "John, I don't think you're the right man for the job." Devine asked if others agreed. Gavin Exell's was the lone hand. It cost Couch a month on the sidelines. At the end of the four weeks Couch told Geelong President Ron Hovey that he didn't want to continue at Geelong. "Just hang around," was Hovey's reply. "Things might change." Thirteen months later Couch was a Brownlow medallist, standing on stage with the widest smile and the purest mullet. He said he trained terribly on the Wednesday following.

"I suddenly thought I had to be the best. I decided after that training night if I go in with that mindset that I've got to be the best, I'm going to play terrible." Blight was able to speak from experience when it came to Brownlows and Grand Finals, having won the Medal in 1978 and lost the following weekend's Grand Final—against Hawthorn, no less. "I spoke to him about it," says Blight. "I just said, 'Look, just play. Whatever happens, happens. Don't worry about it.' But Paul was a bit of a worrier, you know, he did tend to get a bit anxious before games. So, who knows if the Brownlow affected him?" Couch had two hours' sleep the night before the game. "It was adrenaline," he told Sheahan. "Pure adrenaline."

It's possible that Couch's Brownlow also affected Blight, in as much as it sharpened a premonition that was concerning him. For more than a season, Brereton had terrorised opposition teams by running off the line at centre bounces and picking off midfielders—within the bounds of the so-called '10-metre rule', but with venomous results, as Dean Chiron could attest. "Dermott was being Dermott," Blight says. "Running through packs and huddles and people. I just had this feeling. Couchy used to play defensive centre. In other words, he played behind the ruckman. He could read the game better there. So, *everyone knew* where Paul Couch stood for a centre bounce. And I just had this vision of Dermie coming as he did in most games he played, and running through him, pure and simple."

Blight didn't want one of his best players to go down early. What he needed was a plan.

21

SELECTION NIGHT

On Show Day, 1989, the Thursday before the Grand Final, I watched the Hawks train.

Indeed, so spoiled for success were Hawthorn families of that era that watching my team train on the Thursday of Grand Final week with my dad and siblings seemed an annual event—because it actually was. It was one of my favourite days of the year. Glenferrie Oval would heave with people, that graceful old art deco grandstand filled almost to the back row, an echo of distant times. The air carried the scents of spring, cut grass and fried food.

I loved the drills. The players would train for only 20 to 30 minutes and Jeans would stand in the middle, a wispy-haired general, in his club tracksuit and footy boots, his tracky-bottoms tucked into the socks. With the sun painting the sky orange, and 10,000 fans watching on, everything sparkled. At the end of each drill, we'd clap politely and murmur sweet optimisms. If a player did something special, a crisp pass or a difficult mark we'd oooh and aaaah in appreciation. When the ball sailed through for goals we'd cheer, as if it were something more than circle work.

Surveying those wearing the jumpers, Jeans kept a keen eye open for any Show Day showboating—no mean feat with the packed crowd creating a wall of sound. Jeans had learned the pitfalls of Grand Final week when his 1965 St Kilda side fell short after a number of players spent the days before the game ferrying around family members who arrived from interstate and overseas, disrupting the normal routine.

"Jeansy hated anything out of the norm," Brereton says. "So, if somebody tried a banana kick to impress the crowd, or they kicked on their left foot when they could have kicked on their right, he'd call them in."

Brereton says Jeans had a talent to keep players on edge, to keep them striving for better, just with his eyes. "Drills never went for longer than seven minutes, and then he had a secret ... he'd wait for the first error after the seven minutes and blow the whistle. And if I'd made the error, as I jogged in with the other blokes in the team, he'd just stare at me. And you'd think, *he's calling us in to tell me off in front of the other blokes in the team*. And then as you gather in around him, he'd take his gaze away, 'Okay next exercise ...' He didn't have to say anything. Little tricks in his coaching, he was able to get more out of you, with less."

In the blur of 1980s finals success, memories of all those Show Days tend to merge into one glorious beam of September happiness. It's even like that for some of the players. "They all sort of roll into one," admits Kennedy. Although, for me, 1989 *does* stand out. I'd just completed my first season with the under-19s. In a few months, I'd be captain of the Hawthorn thirds. I watched on that night feeling like an insider myself, and not just as the son of 1971 premiership player Ray Wilson, which is what I'd always been until then. But the truth is that, for an insider, I still wasn't very far inside—just one more dreamer on an Under-19 list containing 40-plus names, most destined not to make the grade.[1] But sitting there that day, my premiership dream seemed a little closer to reality.

In 1989, those of us who aspired to run out in the brown and gold had our talisman—a tall, athletic teenager called Greg Madigan. Twelve months earlier Madigan was playing under-19s. But he had been pulled away from that team of hopefuls, been loaded into a cannon and shot on the trajectory we all dreamed about. At the end of '88 he was elevated to the senior list. Over the first half of the season he played reserves. Then, in round 11, he was picked to make his debut against Melbourne.

Madigan holds a special place in footy history for this curious fact. Between being picked for his first game, and actually playing it, he was asked by the coach whether he wanted to give up his spot.

It was weather-related. Between Thursday night selection and the game on the Monday of Queen's Birthday weekend, it poured with rain. Melbourne had a strong ruck division, with Jim Stynes and Steven O'Dwyer sharing the load, and Madigan was picked to lend ruck support to Greg Dear. But as the rain tumbled down, Jeans had second thoughts. "Allan Jeans rang up on the Sunday night and said, '"If we picked the side tonight, son, you wouldn't be in, we'd have picked Paul Dear because of his size and bulk.' I can remember thinking, 'Oh what do I do here, do I play?' And he's going, 'It won't harm your chances with future selections—we have picked the side, it's up to you to do what you want'."

Madigan chose to play. He sat on the bench and only entered the Princes Park mud-bowl at the 28-minute mark of the last quarter, his luminous white arms and pristine jumper declaring his status as an old fashioned 20th man. The Hawks lost by 15 points.

Madigan stayed in the side for the next three matches. His form

---

1   Those from Hawthorn's under-19s list in 1989 who kicked on: Dale Fleming (Fitzroy 13 games 1992-3, later played in Norwood's 2001 premiership team in the SANFL); Jamie Bond (Fitzroy, 1 game, 1991); Justin Crough (no AFL games but won the 1997 Liston trophy in the VFL); Paul Hudson (245 games; 134 games Hawthorn, 1990-96, 108, Bulldogs 1997- 2001, 3, Richmond 2002; 1991premiership player); Michael Johnston (10 games; 8 games Hawthorn, 1991-94, 2 Fitzroy, 1995); Ian Kidgell (3 games, Brisbane, 1993); Alex McDonald (107 games; 46 games Hawthorn, 1990-95, 61 Collingwood, 1996-99); Stuart Steele (3 games, Richmond, 1993); Dominic Berry (1 game, Hawthorn, 1992).

was building. In his fourth match, against the Eagles, he'd had 18 disposals when a collision with John Worsfold left him with a broken jaw. After four weeks on the sidelines, Madigan was back in the reserves, and then returned to the seniors for the shock round 20 loss to Brisbane, at Carrara. In the aftermath of that game Madigan was dropped. The finals rolled around and he wasn't even an emergency against Essendon. Nor was he particularly disappointed. "I'd sort of resigned myself to the fact I wasn't going to play finals," he says. "It was my first year and I hadn't expected to play seniors. It'd come a bit quicker than expected. The team was set, they weren't going to make changes."

And then Peter Schwab was suspended.

Suddenly, the periphery of the Hawthorn team was a mini reality show. A handful of worthy contenders. One spot. A possible place in history.

Ray Jencke was perhaps the most like Schwab. He was 23 years old and had played 53 games (and, in 1987, featured in both Hawthorn's losing Grand Final team and State of Origin football for Victoria) as a skillful running defender. But in 1989 he'd played just 10 games, and on Grand Final day he'd end up as an emergency. No Hawthorn player across 1988 and '89 played more games without landing a spot for one of the Grand Finals. His best season was still to come—1991, when he finally stood on the podium with a medal around his neck. He once hid my pushbike after training.

Paul Dear had played five games that year and been in the side as recently as round 22. At 188-centimetres the kid they called 'Punka' (Pumpkin Head) was short for a backup ruckman, but at a bullocking 105 kilograms he was immensely strong and very good overhead. Anderson still thinks Dear's poor 1987 Grand Final showing counted against him for a long time. In the end, redemption would also be at hand in 1991, when a Norm Smith Medal was placed over that pumpkin head of his.

Steve Lawrence, at 200-centimetres, was the purest second ruck.

He'd only played four games in two seasons to this point, and his best years lay ahead. He was a gentle giant and would be Hawthorn's best player of the finals in 1991, unlucky not to take the Norm Smith. Lawrence is and was a committed Christian, and in his recent book, *Make Your Mark* (Wilkinson Publishing, 2019) he recounts a story of walking the length of a bus aisle on the way to a pre-season camp in 1994 to ask that the driver turn off an X-rated movie because there were players under the age of 18 on board. His teammates had jeered him on the way up to the driver, but there was a respectful silence for his walk back. "It was the greatest act of leadership I'd ever seen," says Collins. "He knew he'd cop it left right and centre, but he did the right thing anyway." My dad remembers a line Jeans said to him about Lawrence: "He's a lovely man, I just wish he'd get two hours of hate into him on a Saturday afternoon".

Andrew Gowers was strong-marking and skillful, but like Paul Dear, had found more favour with Joyce. He remembers being manned up against Madigan for the competitive drills on preliminary final morning. "I thought they'd go with Mad Dog (Madigan)," says Gowers. "Jeansy loved what he offered." Gowers, too, would play in the 1991 premiership team.

And then there was Robert Dickson, the team's smiling, shaggy-haired videographer. Jeans once dubbed him 'Rag Doll', and he was quick and hard-running, brave in the contest. In the 'possibles' team for match practice on preliminary final Saturday, it was Paul Dear and Dickson who starred. Dickson had played six games in 1989, including rounds 21 and 22.

Confronted with all of these options, Jeans chose Madigan for what would be his sixth game. At Marcellin College, Madigan had been a gun high jumper, and with his long strides he glided across the football field. He had key position height, the leap to be a pinch hitter in the ruck, and the versatility to play at either end on players of different sizes. He was a safety option, a multi-positional fallback for a coach who was worried about both the Bourke-Flanigan ruck partnership, and his team's reliance on number one ruckman Greg Dear.

Jeans and his match committee only finalised the team after training on Thursday, so Madigan found out with everyone else. "I was sitting in my lounge room after training, listening to the radio, listening to them read out the teams ... It turned out Dad already knew—he was in the trainers' room having a beer, but this was before mobiles and that sort of thing and he hadn't called home yet. So, I heard it on the radio. Then somebody from the club rang, I'm pretty sure it was Hooky, to tell me not to do any media ... he gave me details about the parade, that sort of thing."

Madigan says it was an unbelievable feeling. "Just bizarre, your dream come true." He says that it all happened so quickly he barely had time to worry or doubt himself. "I didn't have real nerves because the role for me wasn't immediate. I was starting on the bench. The game was always going to take place and play out to some extent before I had to worry about what I had to do." The club gave him some sleeping tablets for the Friday night. He can't remember if he took them.

The only one of the contenders who didn't end up with a premiership medal was Dickson. "For the rest of his life, he never really got over it," says his brother Peter. Dickson did so much with his life. He was the first winner of the reality TV game show *Australian Survivor*. He was a successful filmmaker, a pioneer in making documentaries about AFL football. Then, on 10 April 2009, on holidays in South Africa, he was killed in a car accident. His sons, Gabriel, 8, and Byron, 5, died too. His teammates still struggle to talk about it. They loved him. Everybody loved him. Dickson was just 45 years old.

DRAMA: Seconds into the Grand Final, Hawthorn's champion forward Dermott Brereton is crunched by a heavy bump, off the ball, by Mark Yeates, a hit pre-determined by Yeates and his coach Malcolm Blight. Brereton (accompanied by trainer John Kilpatrick) refused to leave the field and made his way to full-forward. Said Brereton of the hit: "What he did, for the era, was totally fair. I take my hat off to Yeatesy. He didn't do anything that I wouldn't have done to him."

GOAL: Not long after the dramatic hit, Brereton marked in the goalsquare, and kicked truly. He finished the match with broken ribs, and a ruptured kidney... and three goals.

ACTION: Geelong's Darren Flanigan wins a ruck contest in the 1989 Grand Final, against Hawthorn's Greg Dear. Waiting for the spoils are (L-R): Anthony Condon, Paul Couch, Dean Anderson, Darrin Pritchard and Garry Hocking. The Hawks in the photo would end their careers with a total of ten Premierships between them: Dear and Pritchard three each, Anderson and Condon two each. Watching the action is umpire Bryan Sheehan who shared duties with Peter Carey.

↑ **COACH:** Malcolm Blight took over from 1963 Premiership defender John Devine as Geelong's coach for the 1989 season, and immediately instilled an attack at all costs mindset into his players, an approach that took the Cats to three Grand Finals. Blight is one of the game's most decorated performers, winning a Magarey Medal, Brownlow Medal, and would coach Adelaide to back-to-back flags in 1997-98. In 2017, he was named as a Legend in the Australian Football Hall of Fame.

↓ **MATES:** Dermott Brereton and Mark Yeates were guests of the AFL at the 2009 Grand Final. The pair have regularly fronted "sportsmen's nights" to reprise the first seconds of the 1989 decider, hamming it up for the crowds. "He's a ripper bloke," says Brereton of Yeates. And Yeates of Brereton: "A good fella."

THE SIREN: John Feder, photographer for the News Ltd group, captured this dramatic photo, moments after the siren sounded, and Hawthorn had won the Grand Final by six points. The emotions of Gary Ablett (left) and Chris Langford—despair and elation—were replicated all around the MCG. (NEWSPIX)

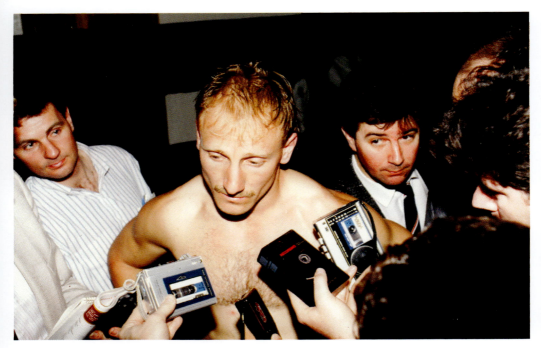

PRESS: Gary Ablett speaks with the Media after taking the Norm Smith Medal as best on the ground. He is one of just four players to have won the award in a losing side, in the 40-year history of the Medal. Asking the questions (clockwise from left) are Ondrej Foltin *(Geelong Advertiser)*, Michael Lovett *(Sunday Herald)* and Tony De Bolfo *(The Sun)*.

SHATTERED: Geelong had fought the great fight, coming from six goals behind at three-quarter time, but could not bridge the gap, losing by just six points. There is no consolation for the losers in the Grand Final as this photo shows clearly. Pictured from left are Mark Bairstow, Paul Couch, Andrew Bews (standing), Damian Bourke, Michael Schulze, and Steven Hocking.

22

THE PLAN

The Geelong players swelled with form and confidence. The team had won consecutive finals by 63 and 94 points, and there was barely an injury in the club. Even Blight's one selection headache—who would suffer the heartbreak of making way for the returning Yeates—was rendered a non-decision when the unlucky Damian Drum strained his quad in the prelim. It would be one change: Drum out, Yeates in. And Blight had plans for his returning player to arrive with a splash.

After the Grand Final parade on the Friday, the team returned to Kardinia Park for its 'polish run'. Monday-Wednesday-Friday trainings was a Blight innovation, moving away from the traditional Monday-Tuesday-Thursday schedule at most clubs. "I always wanted last crack at them," Blight explains. "I wanted the last person they heard talk about football to be me." It was a sentiment that reflected the approach of Jeans, who would call every senior player the night before each game, for one final chat.

Before that Friday meeting, Blight approached Yeates with his concerns about Brereton. "I reckon with Couchy winning the Medal, number 23 might visit him early in the game. I'll give you three minutes to stitch him up—fairly. No fists or elbows. Just stitch him up fairly in the first three minutes because we don't want them ruling the roost."

Still in Yeates's mind was the fact he had missed a state game and had fluid drained from a testicle a few months earlier as a result of Brereton's tactics, and in the aftermath of that incident Brereton had marched beside the stretcher, spitting obscenities. Yeates was well and truly set for the task. "Why would I need to wait three minutes?" was his reply to Blight.

Blight communicated the plan to the group at a meeting in the Long Room at Kardinia Park, under the old Brownlow Stand. The atmosphere was heightened. Aggression was a major theme. Not only was a young team about to step out in its first Grand Final. They had a plan. They were going to greet fire with fire. Brereton had bashed up Essendon in the second semi-final, and Blight was determined that it wouldn't happen to his boys.

James Button wrote in *Comeback* that one player looked down at that meeting and saw a teammate's leg trembling. If the Jeans' mantra in Grand Final week was 'keep everything the same', that wasn't what was happening here. The Cats were on edge. They were up for the fight.

23

THE COMPETITIVE BEAST

On Grand Final morning, 1989, Allan Jeans didn't just take the time to smell the roses, he went into his front yard and pruned them. Blight remembers the Hawthorn coach saying that in an interview some years ago, and it made him smile when he heard it. "He was an older coach [Jeans was 56 at the time], I was a young coach—if you call 39 years old young. I had young kids and a full-time job. I have to say gardening wasn't high on the list of priorities."

Blight remembers playing with kids and listening to records. "Paul McCartney and Wings with 'Old Siam, Sir' was always a favourite. That'd be blaring out. I used to love that song."

Mark Yeates spent the morning washing his car. Some neighbours passed him on the nature strip on their way to Melbourne for the big game. "Good luck for today, Yeatesy!" they called. Yeates waved back. "I told them it was the first time I'd washed the car on a Saturday.

It was just something to do, to keep busy."

Flanigan was dealing with a mini crisis at the pub. "I remember the vacuum cleaner blew up Grand Final morning so I had to go buy a brand-new vacuum cleaner so I could clean the pub, get it open, jump in the bus, and get out to the game."

Chris Wittman lived in Richmond and was dropped at the MCG by a friend. He remembers walking through the carpark with his bag, one figure among the thousands. "It's actually surreal," he says. "It's just the weirdest feeling. You're outside the MCG and you're holding your bag and everyone's walking to watch the game and you've actually got to say to yourself, you know, *'I'm playing today!'*."

Greg Madigan felt the same buzz. With his best mate, he wandered through the masses, taking it all in. "We ended up walking around the outside a bit more to see what was happening," he says. "Like a supporter. Just to hang around outside the ground."

Dean Anderson, in his Grand Final debut, had been awake since 4am. "I slept OK but woke up early." He turned the Grand Final footy marathon on TV. "The first game that came on was the last quarter of the 1984 Grand Final … We were four goals up at three-quarter time, and lost by four or five," says Anderson. "I'm watching it and there's the realisation of what you are about to go into, and the different outcomes, in terms of emotions. I couldn't sleep. Once I was up, I was up."

As Jeans snipped away with his secateurs, he may have been contemplating similar thoughts. The 1984 loss had hurt him badly, 1987 too—two attempts at back-to-back glory that ended in heartbreak. His Grand Final record at Hawthorn stood at 2-3 and he was 3-5 overall. For all the gentle, grandfatherly persona, this was a man whose competitive flame burned white hot.

One of Jeans's favourite activities on off-training nights was to wrestle his players. As a former policeman, he had technique and experience and would regularly beat professional athletes half his age and twice his size. As DiPierdomenico recalls, "People would go, 'How can *fucking Yabby Jeans* keep you down or Dunstall down or Dermott down?' He'd put his body onto an angle. It didn't matter who you were or how strong, you just couldn't get him off. He'd be biting your ear and whispering, 'Just say I'm the better man and I'll get off.' And all the boys would circle. 'Come on come on! Throw him off.' And he'd keep saying it, 'Just say I'm the better man and I'll get off,' and you wouldn't say it and your fucking ear would just be bleeding. You'd could be there for an hour. In the end you had to say, 'Oh, you're the better man, Yab,' and he'd say, 'Oh you weak bastard!'."

He was also a competitive animal on the tennis court. In the preseason of 1989 Jeans hosted rookie players Paul Cooper and John Origlasso on the court in his Cheltenham backyard. It was a stiflingly hot day, 35 degrees-plus, with the Cooper-Origlasso pairing taking on Jeans and his son-in-law. Over the course of an afternoon, the match became more and more intense. "He was getting redder and redder in the face, and he was just dripping in sweat," says Cooper. "We wanted to finish, but we kept winning sets at the wrong times. If he was behind, he wouldn't stop! He's saying, 'Another set, best of three,' and then later, 'Nope, best of five!'"

"We were getting really worried," says Origlasso. "I mean, *we* were exhausted, and we were athletes in our early twenties. He seriously looked like he was about to have another stroke. We were trying not to run him around, but then deep in the fifth set, I hit a forehand volley that sends him wide into the corner and he flings his whole body at it, sending up plumes of *en tout cas*. And then he just rolls into a brick wall and doesn't move." Origlasso remembers the sickening panic. "He's just lying there, almost in a foetal position, and he doesn't move for what seems like ages. Mary is up on the patio yelling, "Allan, Allan!" I'm thinking of my interview on the six o'clock news. I'm thinking, Christ, I haven't even played a senior game and I've killed the coach." Thankfully, Jeans rose.

Here was a man who lived to win, and in football most of all. He had his pact with Joyce, his back-to-back promise, and a personal win-loss ledger to square. Across the football world, everyone understood that a younger premiership coach waited in the wings. For Jeans, coming second would mean failure. Schwab remembers having a quiet chat with him on the overseas trip the previous October: "He said for him personally 1988 had been a really tough year. Not just health-wise but to sit back and watch a team that he would have been coaching, win a premiership, feeling like he'd missed out."

For the man with the pruning shears, the 1989 premiership wasn't just a goal, it was something bordering on obsession.

And now his day of reckoning had arrived.

24

THE POINTED GUN

Blight and Yeates had a moment together as they walked onto the ground at half-time of the reserves Grand Final between Geelong's second-string and Fitzroy's. In his leather shoes, Blight marked a faint X in the grass at centre wing. "This is where you launch from, Yeatesy. From here, you've got the least distance to travel."

The pair had a chance meeting in the toilets a little while later. Yeates was going for a "nervous leak", Blight was seated on the edge of the bath, smoking. "Are you right Yeatesy?" Blight asked his rugged defender. "Yeah, I wouldn't mind a smoke, though!" grinned Yeates as he scanned the butts around Blight's feet. "I don't know if Malcolm remembers that, but I can," Yeates says. "He was probably more nervous than we were. You're a bit helpless as the coach."

As the minutes ticked down, singer John Farnham, bubbling with his own pre-performance energy, burst into the Geelong rooms and roared, "Carn the Catters, I'm with ya!" "I had a real giggle," says Bews in *The Final Story* documentary. "I thought, aaaw, I like Whispering

Jack. I'm gonna go over and shake his hand." Key defender Michael Schulze was less impressed. "Who the fuck do you think you are?" he boomed at Farnham. "Keep it down! We're concentrating here!"

Blight played music on a cassette recorder. *Eye of the Tiger* was a regular near the top of Side A. There was a pre-game speech. None of the players remember details. Blight doesn't either. He thinks it might have been: "It's our time, it's our turn, something like that." It was probably very good, if indistinguishable from others. He was and is a brilliant speaker. There was electricity in the room. "It's a Grand Final," says Blight. "There's electricity everywhere."

In the Hawthorn meeting room, *All Fired Up* by Pat Benatar blared out of a small TV, with accompanying footage of each selected player making tackles, spoils, smothers—doing all the so called 'hard things', backed by an '80s anthem. The video would become a cult item at Hawthorn, passed on to us players in the under-19s the following year like the Dead Sea Scrolls. It set the mood: tackle, tackle, tackle.

As Jeans explained to Stephen Phillips for the *Inside the Battle of '89* documentary (Australian Football Video, 2015): "Knowing that Geelong was such an offensive side, I believed we had to break their game down by fierce tackling, and so we called it 'Operation Tackle' ... We knew that if we got about 40 tackles in the game, we'd have every chance of breaking their game down and winning the game."

Then he returned his focus to back-to-back premierships, the shot at history. "He was really toey," says Langford. "He was under pressure, he talked about '84, he talked about '87, how we'd missed out, so it was third-time lucky." Jeans then went through each player in the team and explained their strengths and why they'd earned selection. When it came to Brereton, he upped the ante.

As Jeans said in *Inside the Battle of '89*: "I told chairman of selectors Brian Coleman I'm going to sool into him today ..."

"I'd been on a flight with Jeansy," explains Brereton, "and talked about my family history, the conflicts on both sides of the family. I had a Protestant mother, and a Roman Catholic father ... We'd talked about The Troubles in Ireland, where my ancestors had come from." Madigan remembers it being "about his family and his family history and moving out to Australia and words that Dermott's grandmother had said to Dermott's father."

Madigan doesn't choose to tell me what these words were. Dermott doesn't either. In a *Herald Sun* profile in 2010, it's stated that in 1958, Dermott's father, "left Ireland in a hurry—Dermott preferred not to elaborate why. His mother followed 12 months later."

What seems apparent is that Jeans knew these circumstances, and by the end of the meeting, the playing group did too, or at least some confidence had been breached. Jeans was a hugely important figure to Brereton—he stops short of saying father figure, because he thinks it devalues his real father, with whom Brereton had a complicated but loving relationship. "For such a flawed man he gave me wonderful ethics," Dermott says of his father, but that fondness is inevitably complicated by memories of his dad's heavy drinking, cocaine abuse and violence.

Mark Robinson wrote a revealing *Herald Sun* profile in 2010 about the cycle of violence in the Brereton family, passed on from great-grandmother, to grandfather, to father. The Christian Brothers in Ireland played their part and the story is all too similar to ones aired here at the recent Royal Commission into Institutional Responses to Child Sex Abuse. "When my father tried to report it to his father, he was hit. 'Don't you dare speak like that about a man of the cloth'," Brereton said, adding that his father was a "very violent man ... not to us, he would give us a kick up the butt or give us the strap." But he was a man capable with his fists. One brawl is recalled with typical wry Dermott humour. It took place at a country football match. Dermott's brother Paul was playing for Karingal and a small group of opposition supporters from Pearcedale were sledging him. It went on and on, "foul and vitriolic," Brereton remembers, and eventually the abuse was directed at Dermott too. With a shared look, father and son decided it was time. "It's a rare thing when you stand shoulder to shoulder with your father and punch on with a group of blokes. But it's quite a lovely memory."

Brereton Snr committed suicide at Cape Schanck in 1993. There are layers of guilt and grief, accusations and sadness that surround what happened. When the news broke, I recalled a conversation I'd had with Dermott the previous year, during the flicker of a thing that was my time on Hawthorn's playing list. We were leaving the changing room area, I'd been talking about starting university, and Dermott said, "Willo, it's funny ... you've got your Camberwell Grammar, and now your law at uni and your nice family in Balwyn. If I hadn't had footy, I reckon I'd be in jail by now."

Jeans played a central role in that salvation. Brereton came to the club as a redheaded 14-year-old, picked as part of an Under-15 squad which also contained eventual premiership players Langford, Russell Morris and Richard Loveridge. As Brereton told Mike Sheahan on *Open Mike*: "I'm 14 when someone came and knocked on my door and asked me to train with Hawthorn. At 15 I'm invited to train with the seniors. My dad's working nights, and I'm listening to Allan Jeans more than I'm listening to my own father ... Then from 17 when I'm on the verge of the seniors, through to 28, when Yabby leaves, I hear him every day."

In those teenage years, Jeans would help with Brereton's commute to Frankston, dropping him at Moorabbin station on his way home. They'd chat, forging a connection that would eventually lead to Brereton regarding him as something more than a coach, "a surrogate sporting father ... who gave me valued counsel on life matters as well."

There was one drive when a young Brereton gave some assistance in return. "He had a VH Commodore, and the car radio had those pre-set channels, one to six, you know the ones that do the double beep when you set the station? Well Jeansy is trying to make small talk .... 'Do you want to listen to some music, son?' and he presses the buttons, 1 to 6, but it's just static and the dial stays locked hard left. He hits the last button in disgust and says, 'Aaaaah, that bloody thing has never worked!'" It was left for young Dermott to show him the trick with the button and the double-beep. "Aaaaaah, that's how you do it!" Jeans said, looking down his nose. He'd had the car a year.

By 1989, Jeans knew what buttons to push to activate Brereton. In the pre-game speech, he not only shared that personal conversation, he finished with a flourish. "I don't know what it's gonna be, but they've got the gun pointed fair and square at you today, son! Just like in the old country. The gun is pointed at your head and depending upon how you react will be how you're marked!"

It sounds prescient, as if Jeans had an ear into the Geelong dressing room. But really, Jeans was just putting himself in Blight's shoes. Any coach who'd witnessed Brereton's 20 minutes of destruction in the second semi-final would have figured that *something* had to be done about Brereton. You couldn't just let him wreak that sort of havoc again. Jeans's speech was certainly calculated, too. He had told Coleman he was going to do it. He wanted Brereton on edge—ready for what was coming. Brereton's last Grand Final for Jeans, after all, had been his shocker in 1987. Brereton played so much of his best football teetering on that razor's edge between legitimate aggression and outright violence. Often, Jeans was pulling his star back, saying, "Don't get reported, son. You've gotta be there for us next week too." Today was a Grand Final. There was no next week.

For all that, Brereton says now that he was "disappointed" and "unappreciative" that Jeans aired a private conversation as motivational fodder in front of the team. As they were released from the meeting, Wittman remembers it being more than just disappointment, and something closer to fury.

"We're about to run down the race, and Dermott's actually at the door. And if the door didn't open, he was going to rip it off the wall. And I remember just going up to him really closely and saying, 'I love you mate, you know, I love you….' It was just emotion overflowing and the vibe of what was happening at the time."

"Whitty told me he loved me," says Brereton. "'I love you, I love you!'"

Brereton giggles at the memory. "I felt the same way about him."

Madigan also remembers the look in Brereton's eyes, his jaw bulging with the force of teeth on mouthguard. "I would have imagined it would be in reverse," says Madigan. "After what Yab had done to fire Dermott up. I thought that he would have gone and done that to someone else, not have that happen to him."

As for Dermott, he swears he had no specific plans for Couch. "He got that wrong, Blighty. There were four of them in there. If one of them popped their head up, I didn't give a stuff who it was."

25

AN AWKWARD TRUTH

There was blackface on Hawthorn's 1989 Grand Final banner. It's a very weird sentence to write, and a terrible marker of the era.

Even stranger, there was also blackface on the 1988 Grand final banner. Back-to-back is an obvious theme of this book. Well, there was back-to back blackface on Hawthorn's banners.

There's no rhyme. I don't think there was a reason. In 1988 the text read "Bring em home to mama" with a Luba-lipped black mammie hanging Hawthorn premiership jumpers on a washing line. In 1989, she was back with a Hello Dolly-inspired, "Well hello Hawthorn ... it's so nice to have you back where you belong."

I just ... dunno.

And for the record, Geelong's cheer squad got it right. A posse of hooped warriors on horseback, with "Charge of the Blight Brigade" next to his giant mustachioed crepe-paper head, a winning combination of old-timey imagery and puns.

Re-watching this Grand Final is a nostalgia blast for so many of us, and a lot of it feels wonderful, comforting even. Johnny Farnham, mulleted to the nines, sprinting onto the MCG. Silvery zeppelin bags bulging with helium cargo, ready to be released on the wing. The old Southern Stand, grey and majestic, creaking under the weight of people. Old style floggers, resting on the fence, awaiting goals, awaiting their moment to flog. And goals. So, so many goals. There's a reason this Grand Final is getting its own book.

But the existence of Hawthorn's banner is a blight on 1989, a sordid reminder that not everything was better. In the last Grand Final of a decade that had introduced VFL fans to Maurice Rioli, the Krakouer brothers, Nicky Winmar and Michael Long, there were no Indigenous players taking the field, an absence occurring only once more on football's biggest day, in Geelong's 1995 loss to Carlton. Eventually Geelong and Hawthorn would get with the times—Indigenous superstars Lance Franklin, Cyril Rioli, Chance Bateman and Shaun Burgoyne were key players in Hawthorn's next golden era—but they were not pace-setter clubs. Geelong had perhaps the greatest Indigenous player of all time in Graham 'Polly' Farmer, but there was a long gap between his 1960s heyday and the rise of the brilliant Ronnie Burns in the late 1990s. In 1991 I played under-19s alongside Willie Rioli Snr, brother of Maurice and father of West Coast's Willie Jnr. He was tiny in stature, but freakishly talented, especially around goal. I was captain, and remember one afternoon at Arden Street, having to ask some of our players to stop racially abusing North Melbourne's Indigenous players, "because everything you say to them, you're saying to Willie too." Willie didn't play any senior games. Maybe he was too small. More likely he was too early. He was a star when he returned to the friendlier environs of South Fremantle in the WAFL.

Whenever I think of that banner, I think of Willie Rioli Snr, and Robbie Muir, and Chris Lewis, men who were racially vilified in an era when such abuse was considered by some to be a legitimate tactic. I think of the barriers that tumbled because of stands taken by Long and Winmar, Adam Goodes and Eddie Betts. I think about three decades of Grand Final memories—Cyril Rioli chasing Lewis Jetta in 2012, Peter Matera gliding down the wing in 1992 and 1994, Andrew McLeod's back-to-back Norm Smith Medals in 1997-8, Port's brilliant Indigenous quartet of 2004, Goodes kicking his match-winner on one leg in 2012. I think of Betts and Buddy and Burgoyne and Burns, and that's just the Bs. I think of their absence, whenever I watch this near-perfect game from thirty years ago.

It's only *nearly* perfect. Never forget there was blackface on the Hawthorn banner.

26

FLOATING

There's a physiological component to running out onto the MCG on the last Saturday in September. "You're out there and everyone's roaring," says Peter Curran. "It's a physical sensation. People talk about feeling emotional, feeling sound—it's a reverberation in your chest."

"Exhilarating," says Darcy. "I can't imagine a better feeling."

"A wonderful, wonderful experience," says Maginness. "You feel like you're floating on air. You come out and the roar of the crowd, it's physical, you can feel it ... you're floating."

Wittman remembers the warm-up lap, the surge in noise as the Hawks turned to accelerate down the outer wing. "The crowd actually lift you off your feet. You've got so much adrenaline going through your body you actually feel like you're floating. And that was quite surreal ... The crowd would lift as you were running. It was quite euphoric."

In a rare quirk of footy history, all three Geelong teams competed at the MCG on this Grand Final day. Although focused entirely on their own task, the Geelong players would have been at least aware of the fate of their teammates in the seconds and thirds. After leading by as much as 39 points late in the third quarter, the Geelong reserves lost by two points when Fitzroy—led by Dean Lupson and a wild-eyed Darren 'Doc' Wheildon, who drew gasps from the Members' stand when he chased down and kicked Geelong's Darren Morgan—went the knuckle in the closing stages of the game. Before that game, the Cats' under-19s lost by a solitary point. But now it was time for the main event. Only nervous and perennially disappointed Geelong fans had time to think about omens.

"The best part was lining up for the national anthem,' says Yeates. "I remember Gary (Ablett) on this side of me, and Couchy on this side of me, and I just felt invincible. That's just the best feeling … I can't imagine … I wouldn't want to go to war, but that's how I'd like to feel."

The Victorian School for the Deaf choir sang and signed along with Farnham. None of the players joined in. Madigan noticed that the man leading the orchestra was a music teacher from Marcellin College, his old school. "I thought that's a bit odd, that's Peter McKenna." He didn't mean Peter McKenna the former Collingwood star, although *that* Peter McKenna also taught at Marcellin and also happened to be out on the MCG before the game, doing commentary for Channel Seven. Rather strange, really, the sheer quantity of Marcellin College-affiliated Peter McKennas on the MCG before a Grand Final.

Australia's 1989 Ashes hero Alan Border tossed the coin. Damian Bourke won and chose to kick to the city end.

The players moved to their positions and the clouds that had blanketed the MCG for the morning suddenly thinned and the sun burst through. The clouds would be back in the late afternoon, but for two hours and 40 minutes, the last Grand Final of the VFL era would be played in brilliant sunshine.

On the wing, Yeates took up his position, marked for purpose. "I can recall standing five metres back from the line, to get a head start, a bit of a run up." Schulze was at centre-half back on Brereton and Yeates noticed his teammate was standing on the near side, shielding the target. He caught Schulze's eye and gave him a 'move over' nod with his head. Schulze shifted to the other side of Brereton. The way was clear.

With umpires Bryan Sheehan and Peter Carey in charge, the ball was raised, and the first siren blared.

"We're set to go," said Dennis Cometti in the commentary box. "The ultimate prize."

27

FOUR SECONDS

It takes nine seconds for the ball to arc into the sky, for Dear to win the first knock, for Bews to rove the tap, for Mew to dislodge the ball, for Bews to regather and get a hurried kick forward and for a leading Ablett to rise into the air, majestic already, and hug the mark to his chest.

Nine seconds, and the day's big-ticket attraction is already lining up in brilliant sunshine for his first shot at goal. It sails through from 55 metres. On the mark, Maginness feels a quaver of panic. "He's kicked a goal, you know, the player I'm meant to stop—he's kicked a goal within 40 seconds."

In the coach's box, Blight's assistant Greg Wells claps the ball through. Then he remembers the pre-game plans. "How'd that other thing go?" Blight takes a long drag on his Alpine menthol cigarette and responds: "Perfect."

It had taken only four seconds for Yeates to get to Brereton. The Geelong enforcer was a champion schoolboy sprinter, capable of running 100 metres in 11 seconds flat, and at this moment in his life he has speed, power, purpose and a thicker, battle-hardened frame than that of his teenage years. "I had to go pretty quick," he says. "I had to go further than he had to."

Yeates and Brereton collided about five metres back from the centre circle. Brereton didn't see him coming until it was too late. "He saw me at the last moment," says Yeates. "He tried to turn sideways, and I reckon he injured his spleen with his own elbow. I got him not quite right up the middle, but on the side, and his elbow compressed into his ribs."

There was no free-kick paid. Yeates hadn't raised an arm and the umpires either didn't see it or it was deemed to have occurred within ten metres of the contest. Within days, the AFL would change the rule to reduce the distance to five metres. But that won't help Brereton, or indeed the various Brereton victims down the years.

The Hawthorn star is completely poleaxed. To his enormous credit, his first instinct is to bounce up, to scramble to his feet. Says Yeates: "He got half up, and I recall his eyes rolling back, and I remember saying, 'How does that feel you weak cunt?' And then he started to slump down again."

Brereton's memory matches up: "I jumped to my feet out of instinct, I grabbed him by the lapel of his jumper and he grabbed me. After that I lost everything, the air had gone out of me, the pain takes two or three seconds to hit and I recognise that it is in my ribcage. I just dropped to one knee and he just pushed me, swore at me, words to the effect of 'cop that', and off he went. And I went on to my hands and knees, then onto all fours, thinking, 'Try and recover, try and recover,' and then thinking, 'No, there's no recovering here.' Then I rolled onto my back."

Brereton says that the most frequently asked question of his career is, "Did Yeates come again? Was there a second hit?" The TV footage suggests Yeates braces for a second hip and shoulder but cuts away too soon. The TV commentators speculate as to a second hit. "Nah, I leant into him," says Yeates. "That's all. Seriously, I didn't go again. Dermott would say the same."

Dermott does say the same. "No, he didn't go again. In fact, what he did, for the era, was totally fair. I take my hat off to Yeatsey. He didn't do anything that I wouldn't have done to him."

In the Hawthorn coach's box, Jeans is on his feet shouting, "Get him off! Get him off!"

"None of us saw it," says Hawthorn's chairman of selectors at the time, Brian Coleman. "It looked like he'd been king hit!"

Lying prostrate, Brereton stamps his foot on the ground. Doctors and physios descend upon him. There's pandemonium on the Hawthorn bench. "It went wild," remembers Madigan. "George Stone [the runner] is on the phone trying to sort it out. Very quickly the message came to me that Jimmy Morrissey was going on, but we didn't know if Dermott was coming off or not." Madigan describes scenes of chaos. Officials yelling into the phone. Confusion. Panic.

After nearly two minutes, Brereton is raised and begins one of football's most famous jogs. His ribs are broken, the capsule encasing his kidney lacerated. Every breath, every vibration is a wracking agony. And yet, as he's walked from the centre, he moves not towards the bench but to the forward line. Club doctor Terry Gay and trainer John Kilpatrick flank him, urging him to reconsider, but Brereton gives his expletive-filled replies. He vomits. In *The Final Story* documentary, that vision is slowed down for full, gruesome effect. "The impact, it's like getting hit by a small car at that speed," says Brereton "Your intestines, your insides go into spasm as a reaction to try to care for themselves. It spasms, and it just throws out everything that's not held down so to speak."

In his head, Brereton hears the philosophies of Jeans: *'In every game there's going to be a crossroad, and when you get to that crossroad, you either step up, or step down!'* He takes the first step. He takes another step. Then he starts to jog. Then he starts to scream.

Says Gay: "We tried to get him off, we tried to drag him towards the boundary line but he refused, he just pushed back, said he wasn't coming off. He was pale as pale, and very much vomiting. making this sort of 'errrrrrrrgh' growling noise, trying to hold his diaphragm down to help him breathe."

Said Jeans in *Inside the Battle of '89*: "The message came back to me that the doctor wants to take him off the ground. And then the second message comes back to me that Brereton wouldn't come off the ground, so I just said, 'Well leave him there, I suppose,' mainly because I gave him such a serve before the game, just push him down into the forward pocket."

Said Buckenara: "I saw Dermott after he was hit, He was physically white with pain. And for him not to go off. He refused to go off and he refused to surrender."

"I knew I'd broken my ribs," Brereton says. "As anyone who's broken ribs would know, any movement is just horrible. But if you can put up with the pain, it doesn't limit you ... so I just started running. Each time my foot struck the ground, I screamed. Because when you're in pain, that's what you do—you cry, you yell. I must have screamed 30 times in a row and most of it was one continual scream ... in the end I just lost voice, I wasn't able to yell any more. Had I not done that, that would have been it, over."

He also believes had he left the field, that would have been it. "They were saying, 'Come off, come off,' but I just didn't, and wouldn't. That was the experience of playing in Grand Finals. I knew that if I stopped, if I cooled down, I'd not be able to come back on. I had to keep going, whether it was for 15 minutes or two hours.'

Blight thought Brereton was just winded. "Yeah, he obviously got him good," he sighs. "If they stopped the game there, I would have been a genius and we would have won the premiership."

For nearly two minutes there is no play. It ends up being a huge delay, and when a free kick is awarded at the re-start and the wrong player takes it, and the ball is retrieved and the free kick is taken again, there's nearly three minutes on the clock. "I was a bit dark he went down in the square and stopped our momentum," says Yeates. "We had to wait for him to get out. And then sure enough, ball's bounced, they get a free kick, bang, goal."

"It's just so frustrating," says Yeates.

28

YOU CHAMPION

It's Dipper who wins the ball amongst three Cats—a frantic slap that sends the Sherrin flying back into the corridor. Bourke bends down to gather it, but Anderson claims him immediately and the hurried kick lands in the lap of Kennedy. He's in space, but handballs immediately because Pritchard is free too. The Tasmanian lifts his eyes. Geelong veteran Mark Bos is closing. Pritchard kicks for distance.

As the ball takes flight, Brereton is already a great of the Hawthorn Football Club: three premierships, 1985 club champion, five goals on debut in a final, eight goals in a losing Grand Final, 18 goals in six Grand Finals, 147 games, 22 finals, 322 goals. But the next few seconds will create a legend and become the most replayed incident of his storied career.

Steve Hocking knows immediately he's too far under the ball. Giving away size and bulk, he's chosen to play Brereton from the front and from the moment the ball leaves Pritchard's boot, Brereton has him cold. Hawthorn's number 23 locks onto the ball and starts to backpedal. Dunstall is behind him: "I haven't seen him (Dunstall) come past me and that means his opponent is somewhere back there too," says Brereton. He doesn't hesitate. He reaches up, chin high, presenting his back to oncoming traffic. His eyes never deviate from the ball. He marks it cleanly, one grab.

It's 200 seconds since Yeates broke his ribs.

Brereton says he never contemplated not backing into the contest. "It's Grand Final day—you don't think about self-preservation, you just see the ball. I just saw the ball."

I was sitting in the Olympic Stand with my father and brother. We all held our breath as Dermott started to go back. When he marked it, the roar of the crowd lifted us from our seats. It was a moment of spontaneous sporting emotion. "You champion, you champion!" my dad half-yelled, half-sobbed. He kept saying it over and over as Brereton raised himself from the turf and went back for his shot.

He still had to kick it. The stadium was going nuts, the Geelong fans booing as loudly as we were cheering. I ask Brereton what it felt like, being the focus of that attention, the creator of that atmospheric pressure. "You hear it about golfers, the great players when they're going for a putt, they can lock out everything," he says. "It's one of the few occasions in my life when I could not hear the crowd. Taking that shot at goal. I was really careful. I didn't kick through it. I almost stabbed at the ball. I can't remember if the crowd was yelling, screaming, shouting, hissing, booing or applauding, That was one of the only times where I just locked out everything. The goal was that important."

Like a great golfer, he sank the putt.

29

THE TRIPOD

Dipper sees none of this. From the moment he initiated the play on centre wing by slapping the ball behind himself, he's locked in a no-holds-barred, WWE-style cage fight against half the Geelong midfield.

It starts with Dipper feeling as if he's been hit by a face full of sand. "I felt like I had dirt in my eyes—like someone just picked up and threw some shit in my eyes," he says. It'd been a muddy winter, and sand was used to bolster the heavy traffic areas of the MCG. Blinded, Dipper seeks justice against anyone within arm's reach. This happens to be Neville Bruns, his direct opponent, and Bews, who gets billing in many of the first quarter fights. Dipper claims them both in headlocks, one under each arm. It's now a tripod scenario, with the Cats flailing and scragging, but Dipper holding on, needing the two legs of the tripod to stay upright. Eventually punches start landing on Dipper's head. "I open my eyes, and it's Buddha Hocking, right? And he's got my head and he's smashing my face in … He fucking got me a couple of real beauties. But I wasn't gonna let go because I couldn't let go.

Because if I let go, I was gone."

When he's finally released, Bews is enraged. Within seconds, he has Dipper in a headlock of his own, a brutal, frightening boa constrictor of a thing. "It was a really strong headlock," says Dipper. "I couldn't breathe. I was fucked. I was, like, 'Errrrrrrrgh!'"

Eventually the red mist clears from Bews's eyes and Dipper is released. Interestingly, when things start going wrong with Dipper's body later in the game, things like laboured breathing and a squeaky voice, he wrongly believes it's the result of the Bews stranglehold.

At the Punt Road end, Brereton has kicked his goal and sealed his immortality. It's the five-minute mark of the first quarter. The Hawks lead by six points.

30

THE FIGHTS GO ON

The next of the fights starts within seconds. Tuck grabs the ball in a surging tide and handballs to Anthony Condon, who runs through the square and overshoots the pass to a leading Brereton.

Then Dunstall loses his footing as he gathers the ball and tries to turn sharply towards goal. Darcy is on his hammer. Enter Brereton, flying in with intent, crashing into Darcy's torso and neck. "I tried to bump Darce and make him hurt a bit," he says. The ball's already out of bounds. It's a clear free kick.

Now they're just flying the flag. Steve Hocking remonstrates with Brereton. Bews is in the thick of it again, pushing and shoving Wittman and Pritchard. In what's turning out to be a big 60 seconds for strangulations, Brereton has a grip on Hocking's Adam's apple. "He grabbed and dragged and pulled at my face," Brereton says. "I got my index finger and thumb in behind his windpipe. It's a Grand Final. People are going to do that sort of thing."

Over the next few minutes, the playing surface of the MCG is not a safe place to be. Kennedy hits Curran with a pinpoint left foot pass, but Garry Hocking makes sure Curran will take a kick regardless when he arrives late, jumps in the air, and strikes Kennedy to the head with his forearms. Kennedy claps in his face as the downfield free kick is awarded. Curran kicks the goal. Says Curran: "It was a nice, big, long, straight kick—good from a confidence perspective because it was no lay down misère."

Don Scott, Hawthorn's Team of the Century ruckman, who faced the tribunal 11 times in his 302 matches, is scathing in the commentary box. "You can't afford to do what Garry Hocking has done. He's given away more free kicks this year than anyone else in the VFL."

Seconds later it's Ablett in the firing line. The ball is bobbing in front of Geelong's goal at the city end. Collins takes possession. Ablett delivers a slinging tackle. Collins disposes incorrectly and is lucky not to be nabbed for holding the ball. Brownless picks it up. He's dispossessed. The ball bobbles in front of Ablett. His eyes are lowered, he's bent forward, and Gary Ayres has microseconds to make a decision. Ayres is a metre away. He tucks in his elbow and accelerates.

Says Dipper: "I remember Gary Ayres lining up Gary Ablett in the pocket because I was running towards the ball and Gary fucking ran and just missed him. Oh, he would have put him in …" Dipper pauses. "I was thinking, 'Yeah you gotta start looking after yourself here, looking at what's going on.' Because it was on."

Ayres, like many of the most lethal bumpers of the era, knew exactly when to strike. "Allan Jeans used to say to us that the time to do some damage on a player was very much about tucking your elbow in and using the shoulder," Ayres says. "When the opposition player is bending over to pick the ball up and when he's coming up … if you meet him with fair force … that's the time to make contact."

This is fair force. Really, it is more than fair force, given Ayres aims for and hits Ablett's head. Dipper says he missed. I'm not so sure. Of all Ablett's many miracles that day, not being unconscious at the seven-minute mark of the first quarter is perhaps the most unfathomable. He goes down, stays down for half a minute, with his hand on the side of his head.

Says Kennedy: "Ayresy was a terrific player insofar as he was able to get the ball, and his hits were always timed perfectly …. He generally kept his arms down, but he'd hit you with everything. His hits were based on timing, whereas Dermott's were more brutal."

Eventually Ablett rises. At this point he is as hard as any player in the competition. "He was just like a tank," says Kennedy, "the way he was sort of hunched over, and if you ever bumped into him it was like hitting a block of concrete. It was quite extraordinary."

"I've just given him a little knock to the head," says Ayres, with a degree of understatement. "Thankfully the umpire didn't see it. If he got that one, he would have kicked ten instead of nine."

31

THE UNDERSTUDY

With Brereton down but definitely not out, ("He got him good, but not good enough," says Flanigan) Peter Curran moves to centre half-forward. Curran missed the 1988 premiership with a posterior cruciate injury. He sat on the bench with the trainers that day, watching his teammates cap off a dominant season, studying the emotions on their faces and feeling, for the first time, the happy-faced pain that is the lot of players who miss out on premierships.

His 1989 season began in the reserves. In round two against North Melbourne, Brereton was still recovering from a pre-season injury, so Curran earned a recall to the seniors. He kicked four goals from his eleven touches that day, a reasonable return. He thought he'd done enough.

When the teams were announced on the following Thursday, it was "IN: Brereton, OUT: Curran." Brereton had missed nearly the entire pre-season and hadn't played practice matches. "It was a pretty clear message to me that an underdone Dermott was always going to be picked in front of an in-form Peter Curran," says Curran. "That's a reality."

Curran knew what he had to do. Centre half-forward may have been his preferred position, but if the main man was fit and firing, it was never going to be. "I could either sook and grizzle," he says, "or find a way to make myself more versatile."

The next Wednesday, Curran began attending ruck training. Jeans was always worried about Greg Dear's workload, and Brereton did much of the forward line ruck work, despite his chronic back problems. For eight weeks Curran laboured on the track and was mired in the reserves. In round nine against Footscray, Brereton was reported again, and suspended again—three matches for striking Terry Wallace. Curran had his chance. "I came in with a determination that when Dermott came back, they'd have to drop someone else."

Curran stayed in, buoyed by good form and the terrible luck that befell Paul Abbott, who broke his leg in round 10 in Perth, and Tony Hall, who suffered a horrific knee injury in the State of Origin game at the MCG. The Hall incident is burnt into the memory of every Hawthorn fan who saw it. He was playing in the red, yellow and blue of South Australia, on a quagmire at the MCG, and ran onto a loose ball near goal. For the Big V, Hall's Hawks teammate Collins chased hard, and dragged him backwards in a typically desperate tackle. Hall's knee stuck in the MCG gluepot, in one of those anatomical obscenities that's still stomach-turning every time you watch it. To this day Collins is haunted by what happened to his friend and teammate: "You're not going to ask me about it, are you? I've just got through the therapy."

Hall was a star and ran fourth in the Brownlow the previous year. In the days after the 1989 Grand Final, Schwab would write a poignant piece in *The Age* about the pain of missing out: "Sitting together at lunch (on the day after Grand Final day) I asked Tony how he was feeling. His initial response was guarded, maybe he was unsure whether he should express his deep-felt disappointment. He then said,

"No matter what people say you can't feel part of it. Last night at the celebrations I felt alone. I felt removed from it all. When you play and win a Grand Final, you are physically tired. You can sit there all alone, but you are happy within yourself. Last night I felt lonely."

Schwab's piece also acknowledged the bad luck of Abbott and Geelong's Drum, as well as his own pain: "I felt strangely removed. I didn't feel like talking or eating. I felt like staying in my hotel room and waiting for the whole thing to be over." He quoted his coach, Jeans: "Football is a game of heartbreaks."

"Someone else's adversity became an opportunity for me," says Curran. Hall and Abbott's bad luck opened a window, and the blond half-forward with the kamikaze attack on the ball stayed in the team when Brereton returned. In Curran's fourth game back he received the three Brownlow votes. Later in the season, against the Bears—the team Curran would play for in 1991 and 1992—there was a potential hiccup when he rose for a mark and accidentally kneed David O'Keefe in the head and released a floating crescent of bone from his patella, but by popping anti-inflammatories and "sleeping with my knee wrapped in one of Mum's stockings filled with electric soda," Curran managed the swelling. He had a great second semi-final against Essendon, kicking two goals from 19 possessions.

On Grand Final day, 1989, 12 months after the disappointment of 1988, Curran is back where he feels he belongs. At the three-minute mark of the first quarter he's promoted—the understudy suddenly expected to step up and take star billing. He's at centre half-forward, his favourite position, and the team has never needed him more.

Curran kicks his first goal at the six-minute mark, a beautifully struck, tightly wound drop punt from the downfield free kick that punishes Garry Hocking for his late hit on Kennedy. He boots his second ten minutes later, a right-foot snap from 20 metres after roving the ball off Dunstall's hands. He wins hard balls in the centre square, throws himself into tackles, and competes in the ruck, using those new skills developed after the nadir of round two. His one blemish is a badly shanked chance running into an open goal at around the 21-minute mark.

It was like the Cats had pulled the ribbon on an exploding gift box. Not only was Brereton still out there, kicking goals, the man who'd replaced him at centre half-forward was on fire too.

32

SPINNING EYES

"My first instinct was to crack into the Hawthorn blokes. It was the last game of the year and I decided, as most blokes did, to let them know we were around." [2]
– Garry Hocking.

Garry 'Buddha' Hocking is a week short of his 21st birthday when he runs onto the MCG for the 1989 Grand Final. He's already a star of the competition, 11th for total possessions that year and equal ninth in Brownlow Medal voting. When he retires 12 years later, he'll be a four-time All-Australian, four-time best and fairest winner in one of his club's strongest eras, a member of the Australian Football Hall of Fame, and an undisputed all-time great. Although he doesn't match Couch and win a Brownlow, there is a strong argument he's the second-best player of this Geelong era. If Ablett is the mercury, Hocking is the steel. He combines fearlessness with the purest skills. His kicking, on both sides, is sublime.

But in the furnace of this torrid first quarter of the 1989 Grand Final, Buddha overheats. He's a late arrival for the fight with DiPierdomenico,

---

2 Buddha, an autobiography, by Garry Hocking with Grantley Bernard (Harper Collins, 1999)

and it's his fists that land. He gives away the downfield free kick to Curran, which results in a goal, when he double-forearms Kennedy with a late and leaping charge. He gives away a 50-metre penalty, admittedly deep in his own forward line, when he slams through a goal after a free is paid to Langford (it's loud out there—we can probably forgive him this one), he whacks DiPierdomenico high and late, wanting to continue the fight, but from 55 metres out DiPierdomenico roosts a goal—a Grand Final classic. Buddha hits Platten in the head three times in six minutes. The first is with his leg and it's probably accidental. The second is with his elbow and probably isn't. And the third is just terrible, a leaping forearm that lifts the 1987 Brownlow medallist off his feet, almost on the quarter-time siren—a reminder that in one area at least, 21st century footy has its priorities right. The umpire doesn't see the latter incident, or at least doesn't pay the free kick.

Here's Buddha's quarter-time disciplinary ledger: three free kicks against, two resulting in goals, and one 50-metre penalty. It's sometimes exaggerated, but the exaggeration speaks of the impression Hocking's wild-eyed efforts left on those around him. Couch told Mike Sheahan on *Open Mike*: "Buddha gave away five or six frees." And remember Hawthorn *did* kick six more goals that quarter which *weren't* from Hocking frees against. But as much as anything, Hocking created a mood. Without his excesses, it's doubtful if there would be the continued conversations about Geelong being more focused on the man than the ball—that they went the biff.

As Couch said to Sheahan: "I said to him 10 minutes in, 'Just calm down Buddha, we need to concentrate and let's get the ball.' Well, his eyes were spinning in his head, he didn't even know I'd said it, honestly. He was just completely out of it. So, I thought, geez we might be in trouble here."

As the first quarter unfolds, the Fab Four of the Geelong midfield cannot get the ball. Bews has four possessions, Bairstow three as he's smothered by Tuck. Brownlow medallist Couch doesn't touch the ball until the 13-minute mark. For Hawthorn, Condon, Pritchard and

Platten are all involved in goal-scoring chains. If the Cats are playing without focus, the spinning eyes of Garry Hocking are exhibit A.

It's not Hocking's finest half-hour. But nor should a 20-year-old, playing his 35th League game, carry the can for the entire team's poor first quarter. It's also worth noting that it is Hocking's enormously skillful pick-up that results in Brownless's first goal, one of Geelong's two majors for the quarter. And he cops a few himself, including receiving a free for a hit that's head high and late by Buckenara. But he's poor by his own standards.

Looking back, we can ask ourselves: was there some responsibility on Blight to pull him back, to get him under control? Or, if that wasn't possible, to remove him from the ground? It would have been a huge call in 1989. In that era, the bench wasn't the place for your best and most damaging players.

And let's not forget the corollary. A horrible act by Hocking puts Platten—who Brereton for one says was Hawthorn's best and most valuable player—out of the game. There's enormous value in that, as reprehensible as the act might be. Back then, coaches didn't tend to mind a bit of carnage in a Grand Final, particularly if it was the other team's players toppling. Take Jeans himself. During the 1971 Grand Final—a benchmark for brutality, with Hudson concussed and Hawthorn having called upon both of its reserves—early in the third quarter Saints hard man Carl Ditterich felled Kevin Heath off the ball. Those on the Hawthorn bench observed Jeans leap to his feet and yell, "That's 17, make it 16!"

In the end, the result of the 1989 Grand Final colours how history assesses Buddha's first quarter, and he lives with that, just as he lives with the defeat.

"God it hurt," Hocking later wrote in his autobiography. "Anyone who has been through the same experience has surely vowed, like I have, to avenge their defeat. But while that losing feeling sticks in your gut, atoning for it is never simple."

33

"IT'S YOURS, DIPPER"

When DiPierdomenico kicks his goal from 55 metres out, daylight is second in the Norm Smith calculations. In game 226, he's played an incredible 25 minutes of football, backing into packs, throwing his body at the ball, knocking it on, tapping to advantage, breaking tackles, hitting targets, winning clearances, laying tackles, fighting. His opponent, Bruns, has barely touched the ball. Dipper is a man possessed, living up to his screamed invocations in the days and hours before the game and ever more: "Born to play Grand Finals, born to play Grand Finals!"

He's larger than life, a cult figure, loud, boisterous, hyperactive, and to use a word of his own invention, "epivescent". In a team full of alpha males, Dipper is the ADHD kid and the centre of attention, shouting that he's the best. It isn't an ego trip—there is a jovial element to it all.

"Hi, I'm Dipper, I've got a Brownlow Medal, I don't suppose you've got one of those?"

"Peter Daicos? Who's he? How many Brownlows has Daicos won?"

"Hi, I'm Dipper, I've won a few cars this year. Do you need to borrow a car?"

Part of *The Dipper Show* was that he was the bravest and the toughest. Dean Anderson tells a story: "We used to cram into this tiny meeting room and watch video footage of the week before … It was all very basic, new generation stuff. Jeansy couldn't manage the technology and we loved that. There was one bit of footage where Dipper was backing back into a pack and just dropped his head *marginally* … which, you know … it's Dipper! It's just gold for all the players. Dipper manages it beautifully, he's carrying on a bit, and Yabby just said, 'Oh, let's just have another look at this, shall we?' He's replayed it six or seven times."

On Grand Final day 1989, Dipper is everything. He is the matador and he is the bull. His description of his sweetly-hit drop punt goal is pure Dipper, mixing tenses and metaphors: "It was a nice goal about 53 metres out. Right hand side. Went through and sort of a bit of arrogance, because you look at the scoreboard running back … the gladiator's running back, his hair's flowing, oiled up, and you get involved in the game and you've kicked a goal off the wing, and you're going all right."

In the next few moments his day will change dramatically. Couch has taken a mark. After going kickless for nearly half a quarter, he's starting to see a lot of the ball. He roosts the ball long, knowing who is down there.

Dipper is in the shadows of light tower No.1. He knows who is down there too. "I hear three words you don't want to hear: 'It's yours, Dipper'." He remembers looking up and seeing the red ball in the blue sky and hearing his teammates call him back. "Not 'it's *yours*'. 'It's yours, *Dipper*'," laughs DiPierdomenico. "Yeah, yeah. OK. All right. And, of course, that's what you live on. You live on your teammates' words and I went back, and I knew what was coming."

Gary Ablett is talking to him, too. The Geelong champion's eyes fix on the target and it isn't the football. He's running at top pace, and that is the *toppest* of top paces. He's a human cannonball. "I'm coming to get ya, big fella," Ablett growls. Dipper keeps going back. He is at full extension when Ablett arrives.

There's a murderous beauty to a famous photo of the moment of impact, an image Dipper will later have printed many times; he and Ablett will sign those prints and sell them to fans who want the moment framed forevermore on the walls of their offices and pool rooms. Dipper describes the picture with a novelist's eye and the DiPierdomenico tongue: "The photo, it intertwines you. Gary's body intertwines into mine like twine running around a tree. He was a hard man, strongly built. I knew he was trying to hurt me. And he did."

Because his highlights reel is so breathtaking, Ablett's willingness to intentionally hurt opponents is lost a little to history. As Couch said on *Open Mike*: "He was a dangerous man, Gazza. He knocked out a lot of people." Like Brereton, Ablett would offer to 'help' his best midfielders with their pesky taggers. He'd say to Couch, "Just float down to the full-forward line and I'll sort these blokes out." One day, when the mid-fielder was being mauled by Footscray tagger Steven Kolyniuk, Couch entered the zone. Ablett arrived as promised, like a ballistic missile, but he was marginally off target. Instead of collecting Kolyniuk, it was Rohan Smith who was out cold. Ablett served a two-match suspension.

Lindner describes Ablett's body as something close to the perfect weapon. He remembers the hit on DiPierdomenico: "I saw the freight train coming ... Darren Flanigan is six foot seven and built like a Greek Adonis, Gary Ablett is six foot one. But if you met somebody in a dark alley ... who's the person you'd least like to meet? I'd say Gary Ablett. I'd rather take on anyone ... Gary would be the last one you'd like to take on. He's a serious athlete in the sense that it's all explosive muscle." "Ablett could accelerate into a bump," says Brereton. "What Ablett did (to DiPierdomenico) was just *merciless*, and wrong. It was spiteful and he knew what he was doing. He got a bloke who was wide open, and he got him in the back. He was a nasty, merciless player to be bumped by when he made his mind up that he wanted to hurt somebody. I stood on their heads and things (in a pre-season practice match during his time playing for Sydney, Brereton received a seven-match suspension for stepping on the head of Hawk Rayden Tallis), but I don't think I got anyone wide open from behind. By god that was an ugly, ugly hit."

As Ablett crashes into him, Dipper hears his ribs break. Umpire Peter Carey pays the free. "You could hear the air come out of his lungs with a whoosh," Carey told Peter Lalor of *The Australian*. Ablett stands on the mark, unrepentant, and says a few words. Within a few seconds Dipper labours to his feet. He takes his free kick, hits a target. Then he folds over, bowing momentarily to the pain. No trainers attend him. He straightens up and shifts slowly back into gear. Three minutes later, amongst three Cats players, he dives on a contested ball to force a ball-up. "In our game you can't look left, you can't look right," says Dipper. "You just do what you need to do."

As for what DiPierdomenico thinks of the Ablett hit? Well, that's pure Dipper too: "If you watch him play, he was very strongly built. He wanted to hurt blokes. Yeah, yeah. He hurt a lot of guys, being hard at 'em. Run straight at 'em, ya know." I ask him if it was a dirty act. Dipper pauses, giving the question some thought, "You know. I would've done the same … maybe, I dunno." And then he thinks a little more and offers his answer. "I dunno. Someone's going back. Grand Final. Fucking smash 'em. Yeah, why not?"

34

I'M STILL HERE

Should someone other than Steve Hocking have played on Brereton once he went to the forward pocket? It's one of the big what-ifs in the 30-year aftermath of the game. Most tend to say yes. Certainly, every Geelong person I speak to, save Malcolm Blight. It usually comes with a caveat: "No disrespect to Steve Hocking..." and "Steve Hocking was a fine player, but ..."

The first goal is excusable. As the smaller man, Hocking is right to play fractionally in front. On this occasion he's probably *too far* forward, and when Pritchard kicks high and long, Brereton is behind him and there's not much Hocking can do.

It's the second Brereton mark and goal that's the killer. It's time-on in the first quarter, and Lindner has just taken a screamer—a soaring, defensive grab on Buckenara's shoulders that is pure 'Prez', and pure Blight-era Geelong. He gets up, shapes to kick and the umpire immediately calls "play on", before Lindner's even taken a real step off his line. Buckenara grabs Lindner and drags him to ground. The ball spills to Curran, who resists the lure of a three-goal quarter and hooks it high and hard to the top of the square—'the hot spot', as we called it back then.

It's a swirling ball, a difficult ball. It's the sort of ball that the better player often wins, because the better player knows where it's falling. Steve Hocking doesn't get a finger on the ball. If it's possible to be nowhere near the contest when your opponent's guernsey is balled up in your left fist, that's Hocking—flailing and futile. With his opponent out-positioned, Dermott confidently stretches his hands into the air and plucks the mark. "I wasn't overly tall but I had long arms," Brereton says. "And I could read the ball."

At this point we're going nuts in the stands. There's another "you champion" from my Dad, who's just barracking from memory. From point blank range Brereton's kick is straight and true. Hawthorn has eight for the quarter and it's 52-12.

It's a heartbreaker for the Cats.

They had him down. They had him broken. "As I keep saying to Yeatesy," says Darcy. "The only mistake he made that day is not sticking his elbow out."

I'm not sure how tongue-in-cheek Darcy is being when he says that. He's serious, though, when he says this: "Tactically, having him [Brereton] standing down there on Steve Hocking wasn't a good idea. He's given a fair bit of height away." That height differential was only two centimetres, it turns out, but again, perhaps this exaggerated perception of Brereton's physical stature gives us an insight, explaining how large he loomed in the minds of opponents.

Says Lindner: "If Yeatesy had have been on Dermott ..."

And Yeates: "What if I'd gone back on Dermie? Would he have got that first goal? I don't think so because he would have been hell bent on punching me in the back of the head. Or I would have marked it. Steve got caught under it. I reckon he probably would have whacked me in the back of the head, and I would have got a free. Or I would have backed into him. You can't blame Hock. I just wish I had have gone back on him."

Yeates reckons that at the time, Blight agreed with him. "Blighty even said that in the bus on the way back: 'I wish I had have put you back on him ...' Anyway, spilt milk."

Blight defends his decision now. "[People say], 'Why didn't you put Yeates on Brereton when he went to the forward pocket?' Look, Yeatesy was a state wingman! He was important in our midfield. Why would you take one of your really good players and put him in the back pocket, when *we've* kicked the first goal? I mean, people say that, and I think ... can you just rewind that? Put yourself in my chair. What would you do?" Blight concedes that the Brereton goals were influential. "There are moments in a game ... I can show you every game ever played, and I can show you some moments, big moments, every game has got them. Bruce Lindner took a very good mark and played on with about three Hawthorn players around him. All he had to do was go back another metre, or just play the game. I dunno what he was trying to do." Blight says Hocking was in reasonable position to run off Brereton, and couldn't have expected the Lindner error or, being fair to Lindner, the umpiring error.

Lindner is adamant he did nothing wrong. "I took the mark and my opponent, Gary Buckenara, was standing the mark. There was a player on the inside ... I look inside, but I don't go. Gary creeps towards me, and the umpire just calls play on." I tend to agree with Lindner on this. It's a brutal play-on call.

"What may have been," says Blight. "I've rewound that a hundred times over. If Bruce doesn't play on, or just does the sensible thing. He took a really good mark. And if Steven was a quarter of an inch bigger, Dermott probably doesn't kick that goal and Hawthorn don't go on a run."

When the siren sounds for quarter-time, Brereton catches the eye of Yeates on his way to the huddle. Says Brereton: "I walked past and said, 'I'm still here, Yeatesy—you haven't got rid of me yet'."

35

MEMORY LOSS

At the quarter-time break the Hawks lead by 40 points. If a team could dream up a start, and have it magically delivered to specifications, a seven-goal buffer would seem greedy and unrealistic. But here it is—a first quarter blowout. They've put together one of the greatest opening terms in Grand Final history. The only issue is the injury toll. Brereton is hurt but is intent on staying on. "He wouldn't come near us at quarter-time" says Terry Gay. "He flatly refused to be examined. Dipper is also hurt and not telling anyone. And Platten is" … *Where is John Platten? Where is the Rat?*

Platten is in the centre of the MCG, over near the umpires. Another Hawthorn medico, Charles Flanc, spies him looking disoriented and ventures across. "John, what are you doing?" Platten has no memory of this but has been told his response. "I said, 'I'm going down to have a shower to get ready for the motorcade'." By which Patten means the Grand Final Parade—*the day before.*

So ends the quickest and most definitive concussion test in history.

Identifying just when the lights go out for Platten is no easy task.

He's hit three times in the head in the second half of the first quarter, in each case by Garry Hocking, and he stays down for none of them. Because cumulative hits tend to worsen concussion, here are the three:

14.00. Platten has his head over the ball, trying to pick it up. Hocking charges in and collects him with his thigh. It's not a malicious act, and no free kick is awarded. The Rat gets up sharply and looks alert. You'd doubt it was this one.

24:50. Platten sprints at a bouncing ball which eludes him. In the corner of the screen, we see Hocking bracing for the oncoming contact. Buddha then hangs his elbow. It's possible he's protecting himself from front-on contact and catches the smaller man high. More likely it's a reckless elbow. The umpire sees it and blows his whistle for an off-the-ball free. I've watched it many times and it's not the terrible act I'd long remembered it to be. But Platten himself thinks this is the concussion blow when he watches the replay. "I normally get up quite quickly and get back off the mark to take a free kick, but I got back up and I wobbled a bit … I went back a bit wobbly."

28:30. To me, the third hit is the prime suspect. First Lindner and then Spiro Malakellis knock the ball forward. It appears Platten might gather it, but it spills towards Hocking, who follows the ball for a moment before rising quickly and delivering an elbow that catches Platten on the chin and lifts him off his feet. I must have watched it 30 times. In the modern era, with 20 more cameras, it would be an infamous moment of Grand Final thuggery. Observed from a distance, it's so fast it's almost innocuous. But to me, it looks deliberate, dirty, and devastating. I really think it's *the one*.

Platten was the finest rover of his generation. He won a Brownlow Medal, a Magarey Medal and between 1981 and 1998 played 371 VFL/AFL/SANFL games for four premierships. In 1989 he was at the peak of his powers. He came second in the Brownlow, two votes adrift of Couch, despite missing two matches with a torn pectoral from the game against Geelong in round six, and despite competing for votes that year with his teammate Dunstall, who'd finish with 124 goals (plus a further 14 in the finals) and 16 Brownlow votes. When Platten departed the round six game, he had 28 possessions halfway through the third quarter and didn't get a vote. In round 22, against St Kilda, he had 41 disposals and kicked three goals, receiving just one vote for his efforts; with 29 possessions and one goal that day, Darrin Pritchard was awarded three.

Off the field Platten was a funny man, congenial and at the heart of things socially. On the first half lap of the first night of pre-season training, every year, he'd chirp the same thing. Before the group reached the old wooden scoreboard on Glenferrie Oval's Brumby Hill, he'd say: "Boys, where are we going for the end of season trip?"

With his tiny frame and reckless approach to winning the ball, Platten would take a battering, and his coach knew it. In the middle of 1987 Jeans attempted to drag him more to the outside. "Jeansy has come up to me, and he's said, 'Listen Rat, I'm just worried about you son … You shouldn't go in as hard as you do, just leave it up to the bigger blokes … leave it to the Dippers and Breretons and Tucky and Ayres to go in and get the ball … just run on the outside'." For Platten, it would mean unlearning something that was at the core of his footy being. "I said, 'Look Yab, I'll see how I go. It's going to be pretty hard for me.' Jeans came back two weeks later and said, 'What I said … forget about it, just go and get the ball'."

"I was his pet, they reckoned," laughs Platten, discussing his relationship with Jeans. On the toughest training nights, the one-on-one Tuesday sessions, Jeans would say, "Rat, I want you to go downstairs and have a rub-down and a shower." "He used to put me in cotton wool, they reckoned," says Platten. "If blokes were tackling too hard, he would say, 'You get out of this, you go down the other end and kick some goals'."

The spectre of concussion didn't loom over contact sports as it does today, but maybe Jeans sensed Platten had taken too many head knocks. Platten estimates that over his 18-year career in the big leagues, he was concussed on average two times a year, or 36 times.

He now suffers memory loss and headaches and is part of a class action brought by players living with the long-term effects of too many concussions. Platten says that of all the hits he took, none of them had as severe an impact as that on Grand Final day, 1989.

"I can't remember driving to the game," he says. "I can't remember if my wife and Mum went with me. I can't remember the warm-up. I can't remember the speech, what Allan said. I can't remember getting changed, strapped, rubbed. I can't remember running out on the ground. I can't remember the start of the game, what the entertainment was on the day. I can't remember getting hit. I can't remember running around the ground after the game. I can't remember getting my medal. All I can remember is that I woke up the next day in hospital."

As for his thoughts about Hocking, Platten is phlegmatic: "I'm over that ... whatever happened on the ground stays on the ground. We've talked about it. I've had a chat with Buddha ... we had some pretty good sessions against each other back in the late eighties ... I've got no grudges, whatever happened." He pauses. "But it happened."

36

STILL ATTACKING

During all the blowout Grand Finals of the 1980s—and there were a lot of them—no team has started as dominantly as Hawthorn.

As Malcolm Blight strides to his quarter-time huddle, this looks like the blowout of all blowouts. As Brereton says: "It's a pretty good coaching effort by Blight. You're seven goals down and you still believe."

If Blight feels like exploding, he manages to keep it in check. He has a piece of paper he keeps in his pocket which contains the reminder: "DON'T FORGET HOW HARD IT WAS TO PLAY". (The following year he gave Ken Davis, a sports psychologist and the brother of former Essendon star Barry Davis, the job of monitoring his demeanour in the box, writing him notes when he was getting too angry. "That was a way I could get better," Blight says. "You started to realise that yelling wasn't the way." Davis held the job until Blight left after the 1994 Grand Final.)

In some ways, Blight is buoyed that the onslaught has hit early.

"I was always a believer, particularly earlier in a game that you still have time. It goes over four quarters … it's a marathon … I've never seen whoever leads the marathon out of the stadium win it. So, it is never quarter-time. It is never the first five minutes. It is the last five minutes where things happen."

Blight remembers his first words to the group were something along the lines of: "Well, I don't reckon they can play any better than that." Then he mentions round six: "Remember how we had them by ten goals early? Remember they came back and got us? Why can't we do the same? There's nothing in this. If there's one thing we showed them that day, it's that we can score goals quickly."

The focus then turns to the next 30 minutes, remembers Flanigan: "He said, 'You haven't got off to a great start but in order to start going forward, we need to stop going backwards, so let's break even in this quarter'."

It's instructive that Blight's instinct, when cornered, is still to attack. *They've scored a lot of goals, so we have to go out and score even more goals.* It's what he told the Geelong Board back at that meeting in Camberwell. There's no thought of clogging the Hawthorn forward line with extra defenders.

Blight doesn't even allow his rucks to drop back. As Flanigan removes his dressing-gown to enter the game, Blight's instruction is to play man-on-man against Greg Dear, who's had the better of Bourke in the first quarter. In the eighties, as now, it was common for ruckmen to 'drop back into the hole' and 'help out as an extra defender'. But not at Malcolm Blight's Geelong. Don Scott even mentions it in the first-quarter commentary: "Where is the Geelong big man dropping back to help out?" The answer is: *back up the ground, waiting for the rebound, ready to be an attacking weapon.*

This is why Geelong remains so dangerous, so compelling. No team has ever scored so many goals in a season. Through the match, Flanigan will take nine marks, gather 15 disposals and get in position to kick what should be three goals. Blight knows his team's strengths and even under extreme pressure, he isn't going to dilute them.

Geelong has ball-winning midfielders.

Geelong has one of the most potent forward lines of all time.

And Geelong has Gary Ablett.

37

PURE ATHLETIC POETRY

For the first five minutes of the second quarter, Hawthorn doesn't get the ball over halfway. In the modern era, it would be called 'repeat entries'. Importantly for the Cats, their star centre half-forward Barry Stoneham finally touches the ball. He kicks a point from 45 metres, a decent attempt, and then has another miss from five metres out on a tricky angle following a superb pack mark. Fortunately for Stoneham, Mew runs over the mark as he makes the latter attempt, so Stoneham gets another go from the goal line.

Geelong has a pulse.

When the ball goes back to the centre, 35 minutes of football have been played and Scott Maginness is entitled to think that things are going okay. Ablett has just the one goal—the one scored in the first 30 seconds, as chaos ruled. "I came in at quarter-time thinking, 'Yep, this is great'," Maginness says. "I felt comfortable insomuch as we were six goals up and Ablett had only kicked one goal on me. He'd only had a couple of kicks, really, so I was reasonably happy with the position we were in."

The pot was boiling, however, and it was somewhat miraculous that the lid had stayed on. Ablett had soared for a mark that didn't quite stick. He was denied a free kick when Ayres bumped him to the head. He pushed a shot from inside 50 across the face—one that he'd normally kick, especially this day. And he gathered close to the boundary only for his flying attempt to sail way out of bounds. As was so often the case when he tore opposition defences to ribbons, he looked 'on'.

There's an innocuous moment around the 18-minute mark of the first quarter where Ablett chases a ball on the wide expanse of the wing and it's just beautiful: the sun is shining, Ablett is flying, and his movements are pure athletic poetry. Maginness is so far back in pursuit that he's lost from the shot. It's like seeing a Cheetah bounding at full stride, alone on the savanna.

Blight could tell when Ablett was in these moods, too. "When he got up on his toes, even at training some nights you could see Gary was up for the session. In a game you could see him, he almost got on his toes. It was like a prancing horse. He was so quick. He was really quick, and he could really hurt. And he could get to full speed in three steps. He was a freak."

Apart from being naturally gifted, Ablett was hugely competitive, a trait he picked up in the epic backyard skirmishes with his brothers in Drouin and never lost. "It wasn't necessarily obvious when you first set eyes upon him," says Darcy, "but he didn't like not performing well, didn't like losing." Ablett was a poor trainer, especially when it came to drills he regarded as repetitive or mundane, but was always up for competitive games or challenges. When he first arrived at the club, Mick Turner, one of his outspoken critics when it came to general attitude, challenged him to a marking competition. Says Flanigan: "Mick rated himself as an overhead mark, and he took on Gazza one-on-one. Gazza won 11-1. Mick never got a hand on it."

Another Geelong gun of the mid-eighties, Stephen Reynoldson, played pennant tennis and could wipe the court with most of his teammates. Flanigan remembers the day he played Ablett: "Reyno had all the gear. Ablett was in footy shorts and Dunlop volleys with no socks." Reynoldson won the first set 6-2. But Ablett began to get the hang of the game and won the second set in a tiebreaker. The third and deciding set was a non-contest: Ablett won it 6-0.

Another time, at Neville Bruns's sports store, Ablett was called upon for what was meant to be a gentle sparring session against Lester Ellis to promote the boxing champion's upcoming bout. But sport was never a friendly jape for Gary Ablett. In front of a stunned crowd of shoppers, Ablett was quickly lathered in sweat and unleashing a furious combination of punches on a startled Ellis. There's a *YouTube* clip of it. You've absolutely got to see it. Then there was the time he ignored the jovial nature of local cricket hero Dean Jones's Testimonial match, flinging himself around the MCG outfield and taking spectacular catches to dismiss Allan Border and Rodney Marsh, before belting the winning runs.

Darcy shakes his head at the memory of watching Ablett chase rabbits. "We went on a camp, out to the old lion safari in Bacchus Marsh. We had this evening activity where we had to get in groups and chase rabbits. When the spotlight went on, five or six times during the hour, the team that got closest to the rabbits, won. To see Gary! Those sort of things amused Gary, and he was just out after the rabbits, like a dog would chase a rabbit. It was extraordinary."

Maginness knew what he was up against. Ablett had kicked 15 goals in two weeks and was in the form of his remarkable life. Says Maginness: "He kicked that first goal and I thought, 'Right that's not going to happen again.' I started hanging on to his jumper a bit … He just turned around and hit my hand away once. Then I'm holding onto his jumper again and he turned around and he said, 'You do that again, and I'm going to knock you out'." Maginness had shared a room with Ablett on a State of Origin trip, so did feel he knew him a little. "I said, 'Now that wouldn't be a godly thing to do, Gary'." At that point, the ball was coming in the direction of the pair and Ablett exploded into his next lead. Says Maginness: "As he's running to make position, he says something like, 'I'm not God,' or something like that." Maginness grins. "To play on him in the Grand Final was a big thrill."

In an eight-minute supernova between the four and 12-minute marks of the second quarter, Ablett goes into overdrive. The first goal comes from a one-hander, falling back towards the boundary line, holding Maginness with his right hand as he uses his left to catch a 50-metre bomb from Bews. With the ball under perfect control as Ablett hits the ground, his feet steeple towards the blue skies and he completes a backward roll. "I actually misread it," says Maginness. "I thought it was going out of bounds on the full. I should have competed harder." From a tight angle, Ablett opts for the banana kick, and his execution is clinical. As fans rise to their feet rejoicing, he jogs off nonchalantly, like a man who knows his work for the day is nowhere near done and accepts a high-five from Brownless.

His second goal of the quarter is a full-forward's masterclass. Shane Hamilton gathers the ball about 70 metres out on the members' side flank and drives it low towards a leading Ablett. Maginness hasn't done much wrong this time. He's barely a metre behind the whole way, but Ablett takes the ball in front of the eyes, at full pace. The Sherrin doesn't even wobble in his hands. For those of us who've tried to be leading forwards, this is the difficult made to seem deceptively easy. "Look at that," Cometti swoons as Ablett's 40-metre drop punt bisects the goals.

The third goal lives in Grand Final history—a ridiculous exclamation mark on an ascending tricolon of football wizardry. There's a boundary throw-in next to Geelong's right hand behind post. Flanigan and Dear lock arms to contest the ruck. "I had Dear under control," remembers Flanigan. "I'm pushing back and I'm going to win this tap, when all of a sudden, someone's jumped on my head ... and I'm thinking, 'Who in the freaking hell was that?' If that's a Hawthorn player I'm going to kill my teammate for letting him jump."

It's *him* of course, and he starts descending from that precarious position up high with the ball in his hands. Now is the ridiculous part. Ablett has no time once he lands, so he's thinking about his kick as he's making his descent. He's at about 45 degrees to the goal and, from a standing start, needs both agility and power to side-step Flanigan and off one step send the ball on a high parabola, clear of the scrum of bodies, away from smothering arms.

The goal umpire doesn't move. Says Yeates: "I remember Gary doing that, and I just looked at the blokes around me, and we just grew another leg … That was inspirational, it reset us, gave us that feeling: 'We can do anything with him.' That was an amazing experience, and I just thought we were getting back into it."

Sitting in the stands, I remember rows of people rising to applaud him, clapping and laughing—the Christmas truce in this brutal and unrelenting battle. It felt like watching a genius improvise, that wherever the game flowed he had the skills and athletic gifts to dominate it. Lindner puts it in these terms: "When you were growing up, you were hoping to be the best kick, the quickest player, the strongest player, the highest high mark, the best set shot for goal, the best snap at goal— you'd hope to get proficient at some of those. Well, he was all of those."

On *Open Mike*, Couch said that it was more than just natural talent. "He had a really good thought process about his footy. A lot of people wouldn't think that, would think he just played on instinct. He didn't.

I asked him about that goal he kicked at Waverley [the famous one from the 1989 preliminary final, where Ablett baulked Essendon's Paul Hamilton at the 70-metre mark, skipping around him with almost comical ease before sprinting away and kicking the second of his eight goals) and I said, 'Talk me through it,' and he said, 'I practised that move on the bus'. In his mind, *in his mind* he's set himself to baulk this guy… that blew me away."

With some understatement, Maginness says, "When he started kicking goals, I thought I was in trouble."

At the 15-minute mark of the second quarter Langford gets the call. He was always 'next up' in the roll call of candidates if Ablett got off the leash. According to Brereton, Andy Collins was next after that. The mere thought of it alarms Collins: "I can't remember how far down the batting order I was. Not far enough!"

38

TWO SILVERBACKS

The full-forward at the other end is putting on an effective, if far less spectacular show. Jason Dunstall is doing what he always does: lightning leads, strength in the contest, a rare ability to push off an opponent and leap almost horizontally as the ball arrives, taps and handballs to teammates in better positions, chasing and tackling, and kicking goals. With Dunstall, there was always lots and lots of goals.

He kicks one in the first quarter, his team's first, from a regulation mark and goal from 35 metres. It's his 135th for the season, phenomenal really. In 1989, he's already had two 11-goal hauls, a nine, and three eights. His first half might have yielded four or five goals but by Dunstall standards he's wayward. There's a textbook drop punt from 50 metres on the boundary that hits the post but then two easier misses that are his bread and butter. When Pritchard kicks brilliantly across his body and finds him 20 metres out, directly in front, he converts to make it 2.3 for the half.

But the moment that's pure Dunstall—the one that separates him from the other legendary full-forwards of the time, and the ones who came before—occurs at the nine-minute mark of the quarter. In the midst of Ablett's mayhem, Bews receives a handball in the back pocket. In an era of very little opposition analysis, Jeans had a theory on Bews and Couch. "We knew they liked to hold onto it," says Ayres. "We watched footage of them during the week, holding onto the ball. We knew our ability to tackle those two would help us win the game."

'Operation Tackle' was zeroing in on Bews and Couch. Now it would bear fruit.

Dunstall sees Bews receive the ball, senses he might try to beat a player, lowers his eyes, and decides he's a chance. It says something for Dunstall's defensive ethic—a trait not often associated with other forward stars of the era, like Tony Lockett and Peter Daicos—that his extraordinary speed off the mark is just as evident when he's tackling as when he's leading for the ball.

On the bench press, there was nobody stronger than Dunstall, and as Bews tries to shrug him, he hangs on with pure strength. Bews is spun in the tackle and disposes incorrectly. Brereton takes the loose ball, perhaps inadvisably as there are three Cats on his hammer but puts it through for a goal from the top of the square. It's a brilliant team goal, one of the most replayed of the 1989 Grand Final.

Brereton knows how to play the full-forward comparison game and injects a little international flavour. "If you were playing Russia in a one-off game, and you wanted somebody to kick you ten goals to win, you'd pick Tony Lockett. If you wanted to put together the best highlight reel, you'd pick Ablett. But if you want someone to kick the most goals to win you the most games and to win you a premiership, pick Jason Dunstall." It took a while for the Queenslander to hit VFL radars. He began his senior footy career as a 17-year-old, playing for Coorparoo in the QAFL. He topped the goalkicking there in 1984 with 73 goals and booted seven in the Roos' Grand Final win. Word reached Jeans that there was a player up north with super hands and lighting speed off the mark. Fitzroy heard the same things. Dunstall, with fellow

Queenslander Scott McIvor, was invited to try out with the Lions. Schwab assesses the Lions' next move, grinning: "(Robert) Walls took McIvor but passed on Dunstall. He must have seen him train."

Anyone who saw the young Dunstall train seems to remember it, such was his ineptitude at any activity that required sustained running efforts. Schwab remembers the baffling first few months. "He had no endurance, was right at the back at anything to do with running. I remember him playing back pocket in the reserves at one point, and we're all thinking *this bloke can't play at all!* And then they throw him forward and then, all of a sudden, *bang*, speed off the mark, and he's marking and catching. Three or four weeks later he plays seniors against Melbourne and he's come out and kicked three goals ... But he was always the worst trainer. And then you got him into a match situation, and he was unbelievable. What'd he kick? A thousand odd goals?"

Dunstall kicked 1254 at 4.66 a game. Ablett booted 1031 at 4.16, albeit with swathes of his career played on a wing and at half-forward.

If chasing and tackling was second nature to Dunstall, Ablett sometimes left the defensive stuff to others. "I used to sympathise a little," says Blight. "As a forward you've got to make two plays. One, to go for the ball. Two, to get past the defender. As a defender, you only have to make one play—straight ahead. To make that first move as a forward, to turn around, you use a lot of petrol. A hell of a lot of petrol. So occasionally it looked average, but sometimes I sympathised because of what he'd done beforehand to get there."

Blight's quiet request of Ablett was to lay one tackle a game. "I ended up having a deal, I just said to Gary, 'The blokes love you. I mean, they love playing with you ... one chase and one tackle for the day ... that'll do ...' And it was so amazing when he did it ... all the players ran to him ... It was good. It was good for him. It was good for him within the group." In the Grand Final, it should be said, Ablett over-delivered with three tackles.

Dunstall didn't need to be prodded. From day one he chased and tackled like a forward from a century yet to dawn. He was the most selfless forward in the game which, for those of us who were desperate to impress him, didn't exactly match his off-field persona. As Brereton said on *Open Mike*: "He's like that green Muppet thing that pops up out of the bin. He goes through life thinking, 'I've got enough friends at the moment and unless they're going to add something exceptional, I have no need to meet anyone else'."

Even in 1991, the curmudgeonly Grinch act Dunstall has perfected for his *Fox Footy* show *Bounce* was already well practised. Funny, yes. Intelligent, certainly. Intimidating, definitely. I wouldn't say aloof, because I didn't know him that well. But Dunstall certainly stood apart. I used to love watching him kick his 100 shots at goal, something he'd do every Wednesday night—usually with Hawks runner George Stone returning the balls. For us in the outer sanctum, he couldn't muster social niceties. He still doesn't. His answering machine, even today, is a three-word drone: "Leave a message!"

"Full-forwards! They're as weird as a tray full of fruit bats," says Brereton. "When you're a full-forward, your total worth relies on *somebody else* kicking the ball to you. You're like the child who grows up in Toorak ... Everything has to be given to you ... somebody has to kick it to you. And that does things to some people's minds."

I used to love listening to Dunstall and Brereton trade their good-natured insults, two key position silverbacks stamping out territory, champions of their era and of all time. But on the field, any rivalry dissolved, and they fed one another, fed off one another, and most importantly of all, got out of each other's way.

Brereton's third goal of the 1989 Grand Final was a perfect Dunstall creation. The tackle on Bews is defensive pressure decades ahead of its time. Says Brereton: "Jason, as a human being, and I love him dearly ... Once you step off the footy field Jason looks after Jason first, second and third ... I've said it before, he's one of the most self-centred unselfish footballers I've ever seen."

39

THE PENDULUM

Geelong is lifting. Flanigan enters the game and creates headaches for a tiring Greg Dear, roaming around the ground with energy. Shane Hamilton also has fresh legs, and is too quick for Kennedy, who rolled his ankle towards the end of his excellent first term. Lindner suddenly seems to be everywhere, winning kicks and taking hangers, often from behind, no matter the risk. There's one defensive grab he plucks from the air just 20 metres out from the Hawthorn goal and the audacity of it is just breathtaking.

It is Lindner's tendency to leap from behind that exercises the frustrations of Blight most frequently, but Lindner knows only too well he'll be praised for his flair as often as he's lambasted for not doing the disciplined thing. For the round 14 game against Fitzroy that year, *The Age*'s Martin Flanagan sits in Blight's box and witnesses the precarious status of the Lindner-Blight relationship firsthand:

> In the last quarter, the recklessly talented South Australian appears high above his opponent like the spire at the top of a cathedral. Even more remarkably, when he returns to earth, it is with the ball in his

hands. The resulting goal seals the match. Lindner has broken the team rule, playing from behind against the wind, but the crowd's exclamation of delight declares it to be the most thrilling and audacious act of the game. There is a moment of silent contemplation, then the coach slowly shakes his head and grins.

But as the second term of the Grand Final progresses, and Geelong attempts to right an upturned dinghy, clangers continue to rattle the hull. Early in the term David Cameron ventures across goal and backwards with a no-looker to the Hawthorn hot spot. Even today it would be regarded as a dangerous attempt to switch play, deep in defence. In 1989 it's off-to-the-asylum stuff. Buckenara takes the mark and kicks the goal.

At half-back, Lindner catches a murderous glint in Dipper's eye and fumbles. Three rapid-fire possessions later and Wittman is running into an open goal from 25 metres. Luckily for Geelong, and Lindner, he misses.

Bews is trying to do too much when Dunstall claims him. The pre-game target of Operation Tackle costs Geelong a goal. By now, the TV commentators are obsessed with Bews's ducking and weaving: "You can't do that in finals … when is Andrew Bews going to learn that the pressure goes up in finals?" It's a hobby horse, particularly for Don Scott. Perhaps it's what eventually informs a widely held view that Bews has lowered his colours on the day, when in fact he plays an often-brilliant game.

For now, Geelong's source of inspiration is unexpected: Flanigan dominates the quarter, but has a simple shot, running into goal at 40 metres, and misses everything.

Finally, in a disastrous one-minute period for the Cats heading into the time-on period, first Bos and then Malakellis attempt to mark when punching would have served them better. The resultant two goals for the Hawks in that minute are heartbreakers for the Cats. When Wittman finds the target with his left foot, the lead is back out to where it was at quarter-time.

After the Cats' strong start to the quarter, when they felt an Ablett-induced wave of momentum behind them, this is 15-minutes of domination by the Hawks. After Bews's superb long goal, Hawthorn score 2.4 to 0.1. The pendulum has well and truly swung back to the leaders. Their half-time margin is 37 points, and it's 21 scoring shots to nine. What's more, there is a sense that had the Hawks kicked straight during this stretch, the game would be over.

But they don't, and it isn't.

PREMIERS: Coach Allan Jeans, proudly holding the Premiership Cup aloft, is carried from the ground by Peter Curran (left) and John Kennedy. To Kennedy's left is Greg Madigan, and at the back is captain Michael Tuck. The Premiership was Jeans's third with the Hawks, after he had led St Kilda to its only Flag, in 1966. (WAYNE LUDBEY)

DONE DEED: Hawthorn had been the dominant team of the 80s, heading into the 1989 Grand Final, but had failed to win back-to-back Flags. Coach Allan Jeans (right) had also missed the 1988 season with illness, but after returning to full health, he took over from the 1988 Premiership coach Alan Joyce. Michael Tuck was playing in his tenth Grand Final for his sixth win (in 1991, he would make it 11, and seven, both records). The Cup was presented by Bulldogs champion, Ted Whitten.

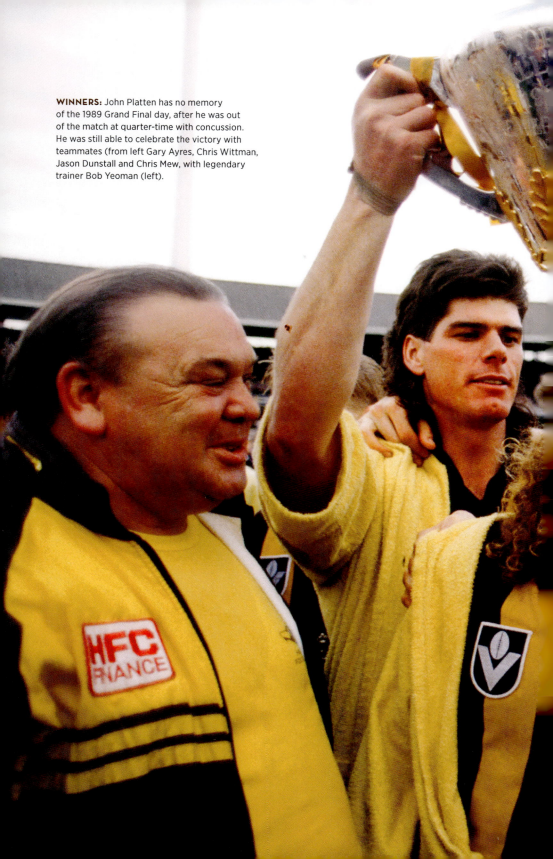

WINNERS: John Platten has no memory of the 1989 Grand Final day, after he was out of the match at quarter-time with concussion. He was still able to celebrate the victory with teammates (from left Gary Ayres, Chris Wittman, Jason Dunstall and Chris Mew, with legendary trainer Bob Yeoman (left).

SMASHED: In a match renowned for the courage of many of the combatants, the performance of Robert DiPierdomenico is a standout. In the first quarter, in a crushing blow from Gary Ablett, 'Dipper' suffered a punctured lung. How he was able to play out the match remains a remarkable feat. He was unable to take part in the post-match presentation and was rushed to hospital, after being assisted from the ground by (left to right) trainers John Howard and Bob 'Dutchy' Holland, and club doctor, Terry Gay. (NEWSPIX)

STRETCHERED: About to be placed in the ambulance, 'Dipper' is consoled by his anxious mother. He recalled his time in hospital: "I really felt peaceful. I felt okay. I wasn't thinking about the game. I wasn't thinking about anything. I'm just lying there, staring into this light, still with my jumper on. Somebody grabs my hand and I thought it was my wife, but it was the hospital priest. Just talking softly in my ear." (NEWSPIX)

CHAMPIONS (L-R): Andrew Collins, Greg Dear and Gary Ayres with the spoils of victory. The trio would end their careers with a total of 11 Premierships between them: Collins three (1988, 89, 91), Dear three (1986, 88, 89) and Ayres, five (1983, 86, 88, 89, 91).

THE TEAM: The official photo of the 1989 Premiership team, taken in front of the famous heritage-listed grandstand at Glenferrie Oval. **BACK ROW (L-R):** Andrew Collins, John Kennedy, Scott Maginness, Chris Langford, Chris Mew, Peter Curran, Dermott Brereton. **MIDDLE ROW:** John Platten, Chris Wittman, Dean Anderson, James Morrissey, Greg Dear, Anthony Condon, Robert DiPierdomenico, Darrin Pritchard. **FRONT ROW:** Gary Buckenara, Gary Ayres, Allan Jeans (coach), Michael Tuck (captain), Des Meagher (assistant coach), Jason Dunstall, Greg Madigan. Photo courtesy of the Hawthorn Football Club museum.

40

BLOOD AND BUBBLE WRAP

It's not obvious to those of us watching, but at half-time Brereton is in trouble. After the trauma of the opening seconds he's had an enormous first half. It's not just that he's kicked the three goals and really should have had a fourth when he missed from 35 metres after outstretching Steve Hocking again, it's that he's rucked, jumped, crashed, bashed, brawled and presented with typical Brereton abandon. He's inspired Hawthorn's strong first half. When he kicked that first goal, it was like watching one man force a river back on itself. "The most thrilling thing I've ever seen," Dipper will later tell Peter Dickson.

Brereton spends much of half-time jogging on the spot: "If I cooled down, I was in big trouble," he explains. He was also avoiding the doctors. 'We still couldn't get him to lie down to be examined," says Terry Gay. Towards the end of the break, Brereton heads for the bathroom. "I went into the toilet, because you hydrate so much, you drink so much, and I start to have a pee, and I'm peeing out blood," Brereton says. Alarmed, he summons Gay, who happens to be close by. Gay is more than just a doctor. He's a past player for the Hawks, having played 65 games, mainly at full-back, between 1966 and '70, a contemporary of club greats like Peter Hudson, Leigh Matthews, Peter Crimmins, Peter Knights and Don Scott.

When they return to the bathroom, Brereton slams the door and pees again. "He pissed into the bath!" Gay says, "as only Dermott would." Gay sees the red of the blood on the white porcelain.

The recollections of patient and doctor depart a little at this point. Brereton says that Gay watched on with concern, asked him how he felt, paused, and then said, "Okay, drink a lot of water and don't tell anybody about this." Brereton adds, "I'm glad that he said that. In this day and age, you'd be off and you couldn't go back on."

Gay says that he never said that line. Or at least not the, "and don't tell anybody" bit that plays so well at sportsmen's nights.

Says Gay: "I said we wanted him off, so we could sit him down and work out the extent of what the problem was, whether it was a bruised or lacerated kidney or a mass in his abdomen from blood, but he flatly refused to cooperate just as he had refused any treatment up to that point."

Indeed, according to Gay, Brereton was up and out the bathroom door at the very mention of coming off. "I yelled after him to drink lots of water, to help flush the kidneys out." Gay says Brereton then burst into the throng of teammates and was down the race, ready for the restart. "He wasn't going to be stopped," says Gay. "In retrospect I could have started to scream to get him off—'You're fucking coming off!' but realistically he wasn't coming off willingly."

Gay remembers rinsing the bath clean, feeling concerned and defeated. "I figured if he was in trouble desperately, he wouldn't be able to do what he was doing—as in standing up, walking, running around, that kind of stuff." The doc was also hoping that the bleed had been caused by a tear in the protective renal capsule, and not the kidney itself. When Brereton undertook a CT scan at Monash the next day, this proved to be the case. "But it was not good medicine." Gay concedes. "Well it was good clinical judgment but not good clinical medicine."

As for Brereton, he is forever grateful that he was allowed the opportunity to continue. "Terry had an acute understanding of what it is to be a League footballer." Brereton says. "The pain of what I suffered is considerably less than the pain I would have lived with for the next how many years if I'd not gone out there, and we'd have lost."

Brereton smiles and shakes his head. "Your health comes first? Your health doesn't come first sometimes."

Dipper also visits the bathroom at half-time, and his health isn't coming first either. He isn't full of his normal 'epivesence' and asks club surgeon, Peter Wilson to reinject a problematic shoulder, for which he had received local anaesthetic before the game.

Dipper sits on the toilet. He doesn't feel great. He suspects the Ablett hit broke his ribs, but isn't letting on, because he doesn't want to leave the ground. His voice, by now, is strangely high and squeaky. His chest skin is dimpled, "like," he says, "it's turning into bubble wrap." He receives the pain-killing jab from Wilson and tells the doctor about the larynx-crushing headlock from Bews. Says Dipper, "Time just kinda runs out. We're called into the team meeting."

We know now that he had a punctured lung and subcutaneous emphysema—where gas or air has entered the layer under the skin—but at half-time of the 1989 Grand Final this is not immediately obvious to anyone, including the doctor. For the team meeting, Dipper chooses to hide at the back of the room. "I'm normally the guy up the front, in front of Yabby so he can fucking see me, but this time I was sort of hiding behind the guys because I didn't want to show that I was weak. I didn't know what was going on. I just didn't know. But I didn't want to tell anyone either because I didn't want to come off the ground."

Platten's history of playing on after head knocks says he would also have done anything to be out there, but on this day, he just can't. In fact, at half-time, in the medical room, he believes he's at Waverley. The culprit is Greg Madigan, who sat next to Platten on the bench for the entire second quarter. Says Madigan: "He kept asking me what happened, 'Wha' happa', wha' happa'?' and I'd say, 'You got belted by Hocking,' and he'd say, 'Did I get knocked out?' and I'd say, 'You came off at quarter-time.' And then a few seconds later the cycle would start again. 'Wha' happa', wha' happa'?'."

At half-time, Madigan walks over to Platten in the medical room to see if he's feeling better. Platten starts up again. 'Wha' happa', wha' happa'?' "I was at the point where I was sick of it, so I just made up a story. We were six goals up, and I guess I was feeling pretty jocular, so I said, 'Rat! We won!' and he said, 'That's great', and I said, 'Do you know where you are?' and he said, 'The MCG?'. And I said, 'No mate, the game got moved to Waverley!' and he said, 'That's great Doggie, how did you go?' And I said, 'Great Rat! I won the Norm Smith Medal!' He was rapt for me. 'Unreal Doggie, in only your sixth game!' Then I left him, and I think he went off to hospital."

41

PAY THE PRICE

It's the story of a boy and a pair of shoes. Like many of Allan Jeans's addresses to his players, it's a message wrapped in a fable or parable. Brereton remembers that Jeans explained his storytelling style as follows: "Every week I have to say the same thing, the difficult thing for me is to package it up in different ways to get your attention."

In this one, the boy works hard and saves up his money so he can buy a pair of shoes. When he gets to the store he has a choice: he can buy the best quality pair of shoes he's saved for, or he can scrimp, and buy a cheaper pair, and then pocket the change and hope he gets away with it. The boy chooses the cheaper option, and sure enough, as is the way with parables favoured by coaches, the shoes fall apart. "He didn't pay the price," Jeans says to the players at half-time, and he begins this message quietly, as many great orators do. "And every day he wears his cheap, uncomfortable shoes with the sole flapping off, he wishes he paid the price for the good quality shoes."

"I'm thinking, 'What's he fucking going on about here?'" says Dipper. Says Langford: "He'd come along with all sorts of ideas…he'd come up with a little story about tennis or dinosaurs or the crossroad sign, or the shoes, and he'd go around the block with the funny story-telling metaphor, and then he'd come back to footy ... and the punchline was always a ripper." Says Madigan: "I'm thinking, 'Where's this going?' He told these types of stories all the time, and I'm thinking, 'What's the line going to be at the end of this?'"

The line is, "pay the price" and alongside John Kennedy Snr's "Don't think, do!" it is the most famous speech in the club's history. Quickly, Jeans gathers his threads. Like the boy in the story, his players have a choice. They can pay the price for greatness and achieve back-to-back immortality. Or they can scrimp and shirk like the boy, and leave it to others, and fail to pay the price, and hope to get away with it, and then regret the missed opportunity for the rest of their lives.

Jeans finds the volume switch. "Are you willing to pay the price? Are you going to say for the rest of your lives, 'I wish I paid the price?' Are you going to live a life of regret? Pay the price now! Pay the price! Pay the price!"

If you've never heard Jeans speak, it's worth searching him up on the internet to see a master at work. I run a speeches site called *Speakola*, which catalogues the greatest speeches of all time, and in full flight this policeman from Cheltenham was as compelling as Winston Churchill or Barack Obama. He did it all so naturally. The variations in volume, the use of repetition, the rule of threes, the slow build using voice and gesture towards a spine-tingling finale that hits on his simple, essential message. Ayres still watches his coach's famous 'Crossroads' speech on the internet. "He recorded that for a DVD in the mid 2000s. He hadn't coached since 1992. And yet it still made the hairs stand up on the back of the neck."

Brereton notes Jeans's charisma. "For a bloke with big ears, and no hair on his head, he was a charismatic man. You could picture him in the amphitheatre of the Colosseum 2000 years ago, and he would have been the man in the middle saying, 'And for the next bout ...' and you would have heard a pin drop, and his voice would have echoed."

It was a voice of power and authority. Dean Anderson remembers an impromptu speech Jeans gave at Russell Greene's 300th game party at Greene's house. "We're having a few cans, carrying on and stuff, and he started, just speaking softly, and then all of a sudden he started roaring. He certainly captured your attention. Very captivating, very influential." Jeans sometimes mangled words and distorted metaphors. John Kennedy Jnr laughs at the memory of one wet afternoon, coming in at half-time, trailing by a few goals: "Jeansy said, 'If you don't change your ways in the wet, you'll become *distinct*. It's like an animal, you'll become distinct'." Says Langford: "You'd look away because otherwise you're going to burst out laughing."

For 'Pay the Price', the mood was deadly serious. Jeans had his key phrase, and he hit on it over and over. Says Brereton: "We were looking at him, and the veins were bulging in his neck, and the projection of the voice, and you're thinking this bloke had an aneurysm twelve months ago … what is he doing!"

Says Langford: "The way he told it, his passion, he fair dinkum blew a foofer valve, he just went nuts. I remember I was standing not far from Peter Curran … and Yab's there and into it, 'Pay the price, pay the price, pay the price …' And he said it six times, and then then he said it another six times, and he's still going, and every time he said it, he's getting more and more elevated with his emotions, and his veins are bulging out of his neck and his forehead. And I'm serious. I motion to Pete, *get ready to catch him, he's about to have a stroke, he's about to cark it.* I've never seen anybody that animated, that emotional, that angry, that loud—anywhere, anytime."

Langford says that the intensity was odd, and almost concerning, especially as Jeans's normal Grand Final mantra was 'don't get over the top, keep your emotions in check, don't get excited. Your performance will decline if you get too excited.'

Despite holding a lead of more than six goals at the break, Jeans clearly decided that his team needed a shot of verbal adrenaline. "I think he sensed that we were down on the bench and didn't have many reserves to come back on who were fit," says Maginness. "I think he was sensing that it was going to be a 1984 scenario again."

Kennedy got this feeling too, and he himself was nursing a turned ankle. "At half-time a lot of heads were down because we were in strife with the injuries, and we're thinking, 'How are we going to keep going with this?' We were pretty exhausted. We'd run pretty hard. We had a few injuries and the concern was whether we can get these blokes through for the rest of the game."

"Pay the price! Pay the price! Pay the price!" Jeans thundered.

"It just kept going up and up and up and up," says Langford. "The dial was beyond the red, it was just unbelievable. You're thinking, 'You've said it, that's enough, that's enough. No, calm down.' Like he was gonna go. So, it wasn't just like a good rev-up talk. It wasn't just like a big half-time tirade. It was not even next level. It was several levels above next level. It was memorable. And I'm sure everyone would say the same thing."

I ask Langford if Jeans went overboard. After all, the speech has taken on legendary status, because Hawthorn was fielding wounded troops and somehow, they found the mental and physical reserves to win. The team literally did *pay the price*. But another perspective is that, post-speech, in a statistical sense, the Hawks went backwards by five goals.

"No, I don't think he overcooked it," says Langford. "We needed it. It was down to that thing ... It was about us just absolutely going to war for that last bit."

"I remember I was crying," says Ayres. "I had tears streaming down my face as I'm walking down the race ... footy's an emotional game and you've got tears streaming out of your eyes ... Yab just had this amazing motivating factor ... he could just fire you up with this amazing voice."

Dipper may have needed actual adrenaline, but this was the next best thing. "Leaving that room was one of the great moments in room history. You could feel the energy. 'Pay the price! Pay the price!' I was rapt. I was running out again and I was one of the first out there, so no-one could bring me back."

42

BANG

It's Darren Flanigan who lines up against Dear for the re-start. That hadn't been the plan. In this pre-rotations era, Blight's theory was that ruckmen needed time to "work into" the game, so most weeks Bourke and Flanigan alternated quarters. The captain played quarters one and three, Flanigan two and four. But at half-time, Blight tells Flanigan that the skipper's ankle is cooked. "How're you feelin'?" the coach says to his number two. "Fine," replies Flanigan. "I just took off the dressing gown and put the thigh pads back on," he says. "And away we went."

Flanigan wins the first tap of the second half, and Dipper grabs the first clearance, his arms high and his wounded torso still crashing through. In the flurry of converging bodies and a bouncing ball, Yeates cleans up Pritchard—not with the same premeditation or purpose he unleashed on Brereton, but it's a mood setter nonetheless.

Geelong dominates the first 13 minutes of the second half. Besides one bad miss by Morrissey in the first minute, the game is played in the Cats forward line. But they squander chances, booting 2.4 in this period. One of the goals belongs to Ablett. It's his fifth, and by his soaring standards of the day, it's almost regulation. Garry Hocking roves and pulls the ball back beautifully into Ablett's leading channel. He marks at the apex and kicks over the goal umpire's head. "Gary Ablett, he is a very, very good player is Gary Ablett," says Don Scott in the commentary box. Like the rest of us, he's already spent most of his superlatives.

In this period, it's the misses that hurt the Cats: Cameron running in, completely balanced; Flanigan hitting the post from 35 metres, unlucky not to receive a 50-metre penalty when Langford collects him late; Brownless from between the goal and behind posts, acute angle, but a full-forward's bread and butter; Robert Scott, kept almost kickless by the stingy Collins, missing a howler from 25 metres. Had Brownless or Scott scored, the margin would have been back to three goals. You can hear the first notes of hope in the pitch of the crowd. The tide feels like it's turning.

Then Dipper knocks out Garry Hocking's teeth.

All day, the violence has come thick and fast, but it's mainly been hip and shoulders and late forearms and errant spoils and vicious bumps—"the loophole in the rules" is how Brereton terms knocking out people on the periphery of the contest. All day they go on, shocking to the eye when you watch them now, in this cleaner, fairer era in which the game's lawmakers aim first and foremost to protest players' heads.

Well, there's none of that grey zone as Dipper unloads. His elbow swings through like a cricket bat to Hocking's mouth.

Says Dipper: "I just ran straight at him: fuck you, bang. And I gave it to him. One of my best hits. And I knew what I was going to do because he was just there, and because of what had happened before, when I caught him punching my head in, and plus he was going around the ground throwing his weight around … He got Rat. Johnny doesn't even remember the game."

I ask Dipper if he'd gone looking for the square-up. "No, I didn't think about that. It's not like I weigh up, well this is his report card today ... I thought, 'Oh there he is, I'm gonna get him,' so bang, I give it to him. It's not pre-intended ... Well, there's intent at the time, but it wasn't, you know, pre-intent."

Armed with this defence, it's perhaps unsurprising Dipper will earn himself a five-match suspension at the Tribunal.

In the aftermath of the hit, the crowd does its nut, some celebrating rough justice, others appalled by an indisputably violent act. Umpires descend with their notebooks. Hocking kneels on the ground, spitting out teeth and blood. "I remember the crowd leaning over the fence on the members' wing," says DiPierdomenico. "Some are going 'Yaaaaay!' and some are going, 'You fucking dirty wog.' I just stuck my hands in the air and waited for him to get up."

Somehow Buddha does get up. God knows many wouldn't have. "Buddha Hocking was a star player," Brereton says, and he says it like Charles Bronson casting an admiring eye over Bruce Willis. Hocking is dazed, though, and his free kick slides out of bounds on the full.

For a few minutes, it's like the teeth have also been knocked out of Geelong. Hawthorn kicks three quick goals, one to Anderson within sixty seconds of the DiPierdomenico elbow, one to Curran, and one to Dunstall. Each man benefits from good fortune. Dunstall is manhandled by Darcy after his strong mark, but is it worth the 50-metre penalty that takes him to the goal line? Flanigan must have been wondering how he missed out on his. Both the Curran and Anderson goals are instinctive snaps, not quite fanciful, but not fully intentional either. Anderson's looks to the naked eye like an utter fluke. Both are the sort of shots where, if they sail through, you feel it's your day.

Anderson laughs when I ask if he meant to kick his. "Andy Gowers said to me before the game, 'I want to see a left foot banana,' and he got his left foot flat punt from the boundary. I was no good on my left foot, and it is the straightest flat punt you could imagine .... I'd backed back, dropped the mark, and the ball just landed in my hands, straight onto the boot, first option, get it forward and it floated through. I knew when I kicked it that it was significant, and then I looked at where I was and thought, that is a complete arse. But sometimes that happens."

43

RUNNING OFF

The mark that leads to Ablett's sixth goal is a thing of such balance and beauty. If Alex Jesaulenko's landmark in the 1970 Grand Final defines the balletic art of the high mark, Ablett's contains the power and poise of a Concorde at take-off. Kennedy is the patsy under the ball, waiting and knowing, and he cops it between the shoulder blades with a force that propels him out of frame, like a comedy extra in a silent film. Then Ablett, soaring, protects the drop zone with those famous hunched shoulders, accepting the mark in front of his midriff. He lands on his feet. He's so economical—a man in complete physical control of time and space.

He kicks truly, and in doing so breaks Kevin Bartlett's 1980 record for the most goals in a Finals Series (21). He'll eventually push that mark out to 27 goals, which in the climes of the congested present, looks like a forever record.

"He was just completely playing his own game," says Langford, "which is when he was great ... When he played well, he was completely oblivious to anyone else, either the opposition or his own teammates. He did not play to a structure, he'd just see the ball, and get the ball, and he'd do things that no one would even think of doing. Because he just didn't think about it. He'd just play his own game, do his own thing."

What Langford did do in the third quarter was exploit Ablett's major weakness, which was picking up a man and playing defensively.

During this period of dominance at the start of the third quarter, the Cats kick four behinds. At all four kick-ins, the ball finds Langford either for the mark or handball receive. "I knew he wasn't going to chase me', says Langford, "and knew that when we had the ball, I had to take full advantage of it."

Langford also does well in the one-on-ones. He concedes two goals for the quarter, but this is a Hall of Fame defender playing a Hall of Fame type of game. There's one occasion where the ball comes in high, and Ablett is in the box seat, revving his engines on the runway. But Langford backs back and denies him the run-up. He then palms the ball to ground, keeps Ablett away with his backside, and hacks it out of the air, clearing danger.

It's brilliant defending. Says Blight: "I thought Langford really got them going in the second half. When we came at them. He won some really good ball, Chris Langford."

Late in the quarter, Ablett is leading for the ball, just outside 50, and Langford is right there in his jetstream. The defender affects the spoil, then Mew gathers and starts a chain of possessions that results directly in a Buckenara goal. It's time on in the third quarter and the lead has stretched out to 43 points. A huge lead. And it's fascinating that no thought goes to slowing things down or loading up the backline with an extra man. Forwards at both ends still have space to run amok. Indeed, during time on in the third quarter, there are goals to Morrissey, Buckenara and Anderson for the Hawks, and Ablett and Hamilton for Geelong. The last of these is a fluky snap out of a boundary throw-in that rolls end over end and kicks up to elude a leaping Maginness in the square. The siren sounds as the ball dribbles across the line. If there's a ledger for luck, this is fortune smiling on the Cats. They desperately need this goal. Even with it, the margin is a formidable 36 points at the final change. Geelong has clawed back just four points since quarter-time.

44

EMERGENCY LIGHTS

The wildcard at three-quarter time is the injury toll. It's not obvious to the crowd or viewers at home, but for Jeans and Hawthorn, emergency lights are flashing. Late in the third quarter, Ayres tears a thigh muscle and empties the Hawthorn bench. Initially he is hopeful he'll come back on. His quad twinges when he kicks long to Dunstall, for the contest which results in the 50-metre penalty and goal. Says Ayres: "I knew something wasn't right. I had no power and I couldn't sprint." So, he comes off and receives local anaesthetic. "Yab said to me, 'Sit on the bench and when I need to put you on, I'll put you on'."

The dual Norm Smith medallist's replacement is Greg Madigan, the teenager playing his sixth game. "I remember how fast the game was," says Madigan. "Faster than any game I'd been in ... faster than any game I'd play in afterwards. I can remember thinking I'd be at an advantage with my athletics background and because people's energy had been sapped and lessened, but that was as quick as anything I've experienced."

Jeans loved to talk about 'faster rates of speed'. "Anyone can drive a car," he'd say. "In Grand Finals you've got to drive a Formula One car!"

Madigan has vivid memories of going from zero to 300 kmph in a matter of moments. For his first hurried possession, he pinches the Sherrin almost out of Tuck's hands. It made the young player recall a conversation with his captain before the game: "I remember sitting just out of the race and Tucky said, 'You're as equal as anyone, it doesn't matter what happens out there, if you think you can get the ball, you go and get it'." Late in the term, Madigan's handball to Condon is important in setting up Anderson's third goal.

In the heat of such a confronting initiation, Madigan has a funny, one-sided conversation with Flanigan. "The game's well and truly on, I'm running past, and he just says, 'G'day Greg'," says Madigan. "I thought to myself, That's a bit bizarre'." Madigan was generally surprised at how much chatter he could hear from other players and the umpires, even with the crowd roaring. "I always thought as a kid, 'How do they hear one another when there are 100,000 people yelling?' But I couldn't hear any of the crowd noise. The player noise was all really clear."

As the years slide by, Hawthorn's injury woes that afternoon will become a thing of lore, but it's important to remember things weren't too flash in the Geelong three-quarter time huddle either. It went something like this: Damian Bourke, rolled ankle, gone for the day; Tim Darcy, rolled ankle, off the ground; Mark Yeates, medial ligament strain, playing on; Garry Hocking, rearranged face, concussion, playing on; Steve Hocking, ruptured testicle (something nobody will know until after the game), playing on.

"I knew at three-quarter time I was in strife," says Yeates. "They taped it [his knee] up, and I went back out to take the kick-outs, but I just couldn't move." Yeates is a big loss. The Geelong veteran is famous just for his first ten seconds this day, but for three quarters, he was also amongst Geelong's best. The injury occurred when he ran fearlessly into a Darcy-Dunstall contest, every bit the tough, courageous footballer.

In the Hawthorn huddle at the final change, Madigan remembers "not panic but urgency" from Jeans and the coaches. Anderson says there was "an awareness about how powerful Geelong were as a scoring machine…36 points was not 36 points."

The Hawthorn injury list is long and star studded: Platten, concussion, gone for the day; Ayres, calf, probably gone for the day; Brereton, broken ribs and internal bleeding, sore but playing; Kennedy, rolled ankle, sore but playing; Pritchard, corked thigh, sore but playing; Curran, knee, sore but playing; DiPierdomenico, broken ribs, undiagnosed lung injury, very sore but playing.

Dipper's is the injury that nobody knows too much about. And, with the coach's adrenaline rising, and the seconds ticking down on his last contribution to this back-to-back dream, Jeans gave him a spray.

It was common for Jeans to target his rugged wingman with a rev-up at the late stages of a game. As Jeans explained to *Seven's* Stephen Phillips: "He [Dipper] used to play with such enthusiasm that he used to run out of gas at three-quarter time. And, of course, Dipper has got a bit of an ego, and I used to always try to pull him back into gear by saying, 'You got me into trouble with the media on Saturday. They wanted to know why I took my best player off at three-quarter time—because he used to run out of steam then. In the Grand Final he was the first bloke I walked to at three-quarter time, and the pressure was really on and they were coming at us, and I went straight up to him and said, 'Don't get loser's limp on me today!'"

"He was a terrifying man verbally," says Brereton, "without ever swearing. He didn't swear, but he was terrifying, if he had you in the gun, and he was yelling at you he was terrifying. The only man who I knew wasn't going to do anything physical to me, but I was scared of, was him."

"A fierce man," says DiPierdomenico. "Don't believe that bullshit the public saw on a Sunday morning where 'the boys played well yesterday.

I can't do anything, I'm just the coach' and, whatever. He never used to throw mud at anyone, but behind closed doors you fucking shit yourself."

Jeans tells Dipper he has to lift. He yells that Bruns is getting off the chain. And then he yells the sentence that Brereton loves repeating: "In all my years coaching, I've never seen a boy die of exhaustion out there yet!"

"He nearly did!" Dermott laughs. "He very nearly did!"

45

THE SCALLYWAG

Jeans loved Dipper. He loved all his players. "His scallywags" is how Kennedy says he referred to the young men who served him so brilliantly, but the coach did have his particular favourites. Says Dermott: "Jeansy privately said to very close friends that he had five players that he loved who were 'his boys'." According to Brereton, Jeans spilled the beans "when he'd had the truth serum, on his death bed."

Anyway, at the risk of sparking team disharmony, 30 years on, Jeans's 'boys' were: Brereton (which is maybe why he loves the story), Platten, Russell Greene, Peter Schwab, and Dipper.

But, to begin with, Dipper was a long way from the status of coach's pet. "I wasn't playing consistent football and I wasn't playing consistent senior football," says Dipper. In 1981 there was a pre-season camp at HMAS Cerberus where Dipper broke curfew, went to the Vine Hotel, then on to the 21st Century Dance Club in Frankston, where he was kicked out for not having a collar, punched on with the bouncers, suffered a broken collarbone, hit a man in a suit who happened to be from Frankston CIB, got locked up, got released, went to hospital, got released again, before sneaking back into the naval camp at 5.00am in the morning.

When a military whistle blew for dawn training, through a closed door, Dipper tried to claim, "a bit of flu". He says: "Next thing the fucking door belts open and Yabby just throws the sheet over. I'm in torn clothes, blood fucking everywhere and my arm's in a sling." Jeans made Dipper do the entire training session. "He made me do everything," laughs Dipper. "There was one drill where the boys had to bump into me."

By 1982, Dipper was into his eighth season at the club, had a premiership medallion to his name, and was playing regular senior football, but not as consistently as Jeans would have liked. In round three, Dipper's first game for the season, he had just the four disposals against Footscray, the kind of return that another coach probably would have ignored in a 143-point win, but not Jeans. The following Thursday night, as he passed through the trainers' room, the legendary Bobby Yeomans slipped him some dim sims, a sneaky scotch and coke, and some bad news: "You're not in the side, Dip. I've seen Yab's board."

"I was fucking furious," says Dipper. "Bobby tells me Michael Moncrieff might be coming back [Moncrieff, in fact, wouldn't return until round six]. Fucking Moncrieff! No disrespect to Moncrieff, but really? He used to wear socks over his tracksuit pants, which back in those days, just wasn't done. Moncrieff! I got so angry I said, "Bobby give me another scotch … and then that led to another one, and another one."

Down the corridor, in the coach's room, Jeans was fine-tuning his team with chairman of selectors Brian Coleman. Coleman, who had coached Dipper in the under-19s, remembers the coach's ears pricking up. "Is that Dipper's voice you can hear?" said Jeans. Dipper reckons he was "about an hour and a half into the bottle" when Jeans walked in. "I've got the crowd eating out of my hand," laughs Dipper "There are about 30 or 40 people in there." Now, however, the crowd went silent.

Player and coach stared at each other. "It was like a western," says Dipper. "Two gunslingers at high noon." Finally, Jeans spoke. "Son, you shouldn't be talking here like that. Let's go and discuss this in the coach's room."

Jeans chose not to use his coach's room, which was occupied by Coleman and was close to the crowded trainers' room hosting Thursday night drinks. Instead he led Dipper to the old coach's room, a dusty, dishevelled shoebox you reached by walking through the open expanses of the gym and up another corridor towards the committee room, and the Linda Crescent entrance. It was a cold and dark space at that hour. As the door opened, Dipper was preparing to argue his case.

"He shut the door and just fucking went belt!" says Dipper. "He gave it to me. It surprised me and then he got me and virtually threw me against the wall. Then he got me again. Then he spread my legs around like a typical copper, got my fucking head, turned me around and put his elbow right in my throat."

"Now listen son," Jeans said, according to Dipper. "I don't bloody care what you bloody do, but you have disgraced yourself, you've disgraced the football club, you've disgraced your family. Who do you think you are?"

Dipper started crying. Big heaving sobs that his teammates enjoy re-enacting. He cried and cried and made promises to Jeans to do better. He'd party less, train harder, obey the rules, prove himself to Jeans as a person and a footballer.

Dipper didn't play his next senior game until nine rounds later. Just over a year later, he'd have a second premiership medallion and, within four years, a Brownlow. In 1989 he played every game and was close to best on ground at quarter-time of the Grand Final. But at three-quarter time, Jeans eyed him up. "Bruns is starting to get on the bike. You got to get on the bike, Robert. Keep running son, run, run, run!"

46

BROKEN BODIES

At three-quarter time, Jeans also tells Wittman and Condon to share roving duties. "Platts is gone, so it's up to you boys," the coach says. Wittman recalls: "I remember turning to Condo and saying, 'You start', and he turned to me and said, 'You start', because we were both so exhausted."

Condon ends up heading to the centre of the ground. Buckenara is there too. Wittman goes to the forward flank, where he's picked up by Buddha Hocking. "I looked at Hocking, and I could have pushed him over with a feather," Wittman says. "His eyes were rolling back in his head. He was frothing at the mouth. He had concussion, which I didn't understand until after the game—that he'd got belted. I just looked at him, and thought, 'We can do this,' because he didn't even know where he was."

The ball is bounced to begin what will be 30 of the most exhilarating minutes of football ever played. Buckenara finds Anderson, who finds Dunstall in the first minute, and the Cats are deep into their ninth life.

"If he gets this the Grand Final should be all over," says Cometti.

But as the Sword of Damocles drops…Dunstall misses.

Next Wittman himself has a chance to finish the Cats. His right foot snap falls short. Dunstall almost marks the kick. Bews clears. Then Anderson has a go. He's 40 metres out, in space. The way he's been hitting them, you'd back him in. He misses to the right. Three shots in two minutes. Any one of them would have been the executioner's bullet. Meanwhile, Hawthorn's injury woes have worsened. In the first minute Tuck tackles Bairstow and splits the webbing between the middle and ring fingers of his left hand. Says Tuck: "If there had have been a blood rule in those days, I would have been off, and we would have been down to 17 men." Instead Hawks runner George Stone signals frantically for tape. Later Tuck will receive seven stitches, the sort of wound in civilian life that has us wincing and whinging for a month. In less than a minute the Hawthorn skipper stems the bleeding and return to the game. He's tagged Bairstow brilliantly for three quarters. There's 28 minutes to go and a job is still to be done.

Now it's Geelong's turn to attack and for two minutes it's a desperate Langford with his finger in the dyke. Firstly, he flies alongside Ablett, his Christopher Reeve jawline going up against the footballing Superman. Langford takes a superb mark from the front. Seconds later they're at it again on the goal line, Ablett in one of his favourite positions, pushing hard with one elbow, attempting to curl in the one-hander. Langford punches it through for a behind.

At the three-minute mark, Yeates hobbles off, finished for the day by his knee injury. That brings the hobbling Darcy back onto the ground, a man who should also be finished. With nearly the entire final quarter still to play out, there are no more interchange options for either team.

Brereton is still competing hard but appears cooked. Darcy limps over to pick him up but he is cooked too. There's a desperate but weary contest on Hawthorn's half-forward line, where Brereton rattles his broken ribs with a diving belly-flop, but he drops the mark, Darcy picks it up, Dipper tackles him, the ball spills, Brereton handballs, and

Dipper and Darcy force it out of bounds. Broken bodies everywhere, nobody yielding.

Geelong finally get the first goal for the quarter and it's another party trick from Ablett. This time it isn't Ablett who finishes it off, but in the lead-up he holds Langford out, drops the one hander, hares off after it, paddles it to himself, picks up the ball and almost flick-passes as he dives forward. His lightning handball finds Scott, who finds Bruns, who slots it from 20 metres.

For Ablett aficionados, he finishes up sitting on the ground in the same pocket as the "what more can you say?" goal against Collingwood, which may be the greatest individual goal of all time. This assist is not quite at that level, but nobody else on the ground could have done it.

The margin is back to 29 points.

47

THE ACHILLES HEEL

The problem for Geelong now is the one that haunts them all afternoon. It may even be the Achilles heel of Blight-era Geelong. The Cats cannot stop a quality forward line from kicking goals. Says Langford: "They always had the talent, and they were very good at kicking high scores, but their defence leaked like sieve, and their midfield leaked too." Brereton agrees: "Geelong's forward line might have been the greatest collection of key position talent we've ever seen … but their back end was cobbled together. Blight always wanted to turn it into a shootout, but they weren't brilliant at the back end."

After the Bruns goal, it's so important that Hawthorn doesn't get the next one. The charge of the Blight Brigade has little space in which to manoeuvre, and it needs to start its move now. Instead the tired Hawks rally. Wittman is back in for the centre bounce and quickly wins one of the most important clearances of his career. It starts a chain in which Morrissey, the man Hawthorn diehards call "The Freak", takes a one-hander—a superb piece of skill—and handballs immediately to a running

Pritchard who chips a delicate 15-metre ball to Buckenara. Buckenara is in acres of space at centre half-forward, and is half turning his body towards goal even as the ball is still arriving. He plays on immediately, all alone and completely balanced, and kicks truly. The margin is back to 35 points.

Buckenara's opponent at this point is Bruce Lindner. It's the Hawthorn champ's fourth goal for the game, and every Cats fan is screaming, 'Who's on him?' Lindner is a creative force this day, running off half-back. He marks everything, weaves in and out of packs and hits his targets continually. After Ablett and Flanigan, the temptation is to say he's Geelong's next best, although Bews, Bos, Couch and Hamilton are in that conversation too. The problem, as ever, is the defensive side of his game. Buckenara ends up with 20 disposals for the day and kicks his four goals. Lindner also spends time on Anderson, who also boots four. "Bruce had a theory that if you could see them, you were manned up," laughs his close friend Flanigan. "How many did he have kicked on him? Was it about eight?"

Lindner says it was five: "I'll put my hand up for three of them. One was a turnover and one was a player standing in the goal square who I had to leave to run out."

48

IT'S ALL HAPPENING

There are dramatic story arcs emerging all over the ground. The ball is kicked long to Brownless, and running back with the flight, his opponent Maginness slams into the behind post with his neck. The Hawk holds the mark, which, as a piece of skill under pressure, is just phenomenal. But the padding on the point posts of the era is too skimpy for such a battering, and Maginness is lifted off his feet by the force. The defender lies flat on the ground, legs twitching. Slowly, he gets up and takes his kick. "I was tender for a few weeks," says Maginness. But he stays out there. Everyone must stay out there.

From here, Geelong kicks behinds when they so desperately need goals. Bews misses from distance, Hamilton from a left-foot banana, under pressure, but from just a few metres out, and Malakellis from a 40-metre set shot—one he should have nailed. The kick out is marked by Bruns. Boos ring out across the MCG. For four years Hawthorn fans have booed Bruns for having the temerity to let his jaw be broken in an unprovoked, off-the-ball attack by Leigh Matthews, during an infamously hostile game at Princes Park in 1985. Bruns's Grand Final has been quiet, and he's beaten by Dipper, but his career resurrection has been commendable: Shattered both physically and emotionally by the Matthews incident, the nuggetty rover went from the fringe of State selection to the Geelong reserves within a year. Facing the prospect of early retirement, Bruns instead reinvented himself as a wingman, determined not to be remembered merely as the poor sap who was belted by Lethal.

Bruns's kick to Flanigan is a study in precision. It's the ruckman's eighth mark and 13th kick since entering the game at quarter-time. He's run rampant, really, on top in the ruck contests against Dear, and simply everywhere in Geelong's chains of possession. As he lines up, he's outside the 50-metre arc. "Was it 80?" laughs Flanigan. "Nah, 45 with the wind. But as the years go by it gets further and further."

It's a beautiful kick. He probably kicks it from 52 metres out and it nearly clears the fence.

Just seconds later the ball is in Ablett's hands after he leads and marks in one of his few regulation plays for the day. Langford has been drawn to the ball and has allowed the elastic band to stretch. Ablett kicks straight for his seventh. On this day, he only kicks straight. It makes Collins think of a team meeting early on the Friday, when Jeans was numbering off the defenders who might get the Ablett job. "I remember Peter Curran, a forward, mind you ... PC chimed in and said, 'You don't have to worry about Ablett. He won't hurt us. He's not a straight kick at goal.' We laughed then, we're still laughing now. What'd he kick? Was it nine straight?"

It was 9.1. In fairness to Curran, the previous two weeks had been 8.5 and 7.7. Plenty of behinds there!

If one of the glories of Australian Rules football is the 360-degree field of possibility, Langford says the lot of the full-back is reducing that to a manageable wedge. "You try and marginalise." Langford explains. "Reduce the number of options an opponent has ... If you can cover 270 degrees of his options, and the other 90 degrees that he's got left is out to the side or out to the boundary line or whatever, then that's all you can do. I think most of the time, with Ablett, that's what I did. The unfortunate part of it is that he used his 90 degrees and he was still able to do something extraordinary with it. You gave him very limited options, and yet he's still able to get the ball, win it, and then somehow kick a goal from places he shouldn't be kicking them. He was so freakish and unpredictable. I think I won a few contests by taking the obvious option, and he won a few by taking the least obvious option."

There's one image that's on my podium for the most thrilling moment of this extraordinary Grand Final. It's a little over 10 minutes into the final quarter. Bews gathers the ball after a big knock from Dear, then handballs to Bruns, and Bruns kicks high and long.

"I was sitting in the hole," says Madigan. "I remember the ball getting popped up and I thought, 'Oh hell, here we are. I'm just the stepladder for him. I'm going to be Phil Baker's Kelvin Moore or Jezza's Jerker Jenkin. I'll be on every poster, just spread-eagled while Ablett is on my head.' I could hear the crowd then. The crowd went nuts."

Madigan is right to be worried. Ablett is coming, and he is in the mood for flying. He launches and Madigan collapses forward. Ablett's legs almost wrap around the young Hawk's head, and now Superman is horizontal to the ground, fully extended about three metres in the air.

"I can remember the crowd," says Langford. "They were all obviously riding the Gary Ablett ticket, and they saw him jump and he had that spectacular way of doing it, and they got really excited by that and they saw two hands on the ball and they go, 'How good's that?' And all of a sudden the pack's come down and the ball is in my two hands."

It's one of the most extraordinary marks I've ever seen. Ablett soars and looks like he has it, but Langford has spotted that his opponent is slightly under the ball and takes a strong, if regulation, overhead mark. He lands on his feet. "I realised he'd jumped and that he was not at the highest point and I could get higher, and so made the call to go for the mark," Langford says. "Thankfully I hung onto it."

Things now start getting crazy. In the seconds following the

Langford mark a streaker hits the field dressed as Batwoman. She's the first Grand Final streaker since Helen D'Amico in 1982, but whereas D'Amico had time to flirt and frolic, Batwoman correctly reads the pace of the game, sprinting at full clip towards the centre of the MCG—all cape and cowl and not much else.

"I remember running towards the members' wing," says Flanigan, "when all of a sudden I see this Caped Crusader flying across the ground. I reckon I missed her by about two metres. It would have been interesting if I collided into her and got injured."

When I explain to people that the 1989 Grand Final is the greatest game ever played, I often think of 100,000 people being so gripped by the football that they ignored Catwoman.

There's a lesson in this for exhibitionists: streak in quiet patches of boring Grand Finals.

49

OTHER COURAGE

I ask Chris Wittman about the other type of courage, the type that's perhaps less obvious than Mark Yeates backing into a pack, or Dermott Brereton kicking his Lazarus goal. It's the courage to keep running, to run at maximum effort and to seek further lactic pain, to bully your own brain into continuing to punish the body. "Whatever you've got left in your petrol tank, that's what you're trying to contribute," Wittman says. "I was exhausted to the point where I couldn't kick 50 metres anymore. So, I was getting the ball out of packs, I was kicking it short to teammates or I was laying a tackle."

At the 12-minute mark of the final quarter, with Geelong charging and Catwoman cavorting, Wittman lunges for a tackle that will enter the fine print of how the game was won. Couch has the ball—after his shocking first quarter, the Brownlow medallist lifted and became a terrific contributor—but he sees a wall of Hawthorn players, and with his considerable evasive talent, dummies a handball while accelerating towards the gap. Wittman props, corrals, chases, lunges, and just as it appears Couch is home free, Wittman catches his waist and drags him to ground. Couch disposes incorrectly, Curran gathers and accepts the play-on advantage, then swings onto his right foot and kicks to the perfect spot for Dunstall to do his Dunstall thing. He kicks straight for his fourth.

Again, it's a goal against the tide.

Says Brereton: "The amazing thing about that Grand Final is there was a lot of heavy lifting at the start—Dipper, Yeatesy and I, Buddha Hocking—but when Hawthorn was dead on its feet, four blokes played the most meaningful 30 minutes of football in their lives. And they were Dean Anderson, Darrin Pritchard, Chris Wittman and Gary Buckenara. They were the ones who kept running and kept us in the game. No matter what had been done in the first three quarters, without those four, we lose."

Geelong responds within a minute. It's Flanigan again, setting up behind the ball, and then finding Stoneham on the 50. Stoneham's kick is a beauty. The margin is back to 21 points again, and we're less than halfway through the final quarter.

For the next five minutes it feels like the mad ball phase of a pinball game. Bodies collide, possession swings from one team to another, the ball flies from end to end. Morrissey slaloms through a pack and rolls the ball up his arm like a Harlem Globetrotter. If he kicks truly with his left foot snap, it'll be replayed for all time. He misses by a metre. Dipper misses too, after Lindner fails to stop him playing on. On the TV, there's a shot of a Hawthorn supporter in the crowd openly sobbing, the September sun lighting up her eighties perm, her heightened emotional state reflecting the atmosphere throughout the stands. Ablett looks set for another screamer, but this time doesn't get lift-off. Could he possibly be tiring? On the outer wing the teams arm-wrestle—14 possessions in 45 seconds as players throw themselves at each other and the ball.

The violent acts of the first three quarters have dissipated, as players channel their remaining energy into getting and keeping the ball. There is now pure focus on the ball and the prize. When nostalgia buffs tell you footy was better before 'defensive structures', this is what they mean.

50

THE MIRACLE MAN

Ablett's eighth is his most beautiful. Again, Lindner breaks the line, spinning out of half-back and bouncing through the centre. He kicks long and wide for the Miracle Man. "They just went to Gary at every opportunity," says Maginness, who by this point has the job on Brownless. "There were times when Billy was clear, when he was definitely the right option for a kick inside 50, and they'd just ignore him and kick it straight to Gary, who had Langers laying in on him all the time."

Langford is in perfect position and they're both running flat out, virtually side by side. As the ball arrives, Ablett levers him under the flight with his right elbow and drops the mark with his left hand. But before the ball hits the ground he's already spun, like a weathervane on a barn, and suddenly he's facing the opposite way, collecting with his right hand as Langford continues along the straight line. He now has time and space, and calmly places the ball across his left boot and snaps truly. In fast motion it's mesmerising. His decision to go one-handed, first in the marking contest and then to change hands as he collects his own crumb, is essential to the speed of the turn and the economy of his movement. I've just watched it twenty times. It's football poetry. He's not even a left footer.

"He's the most explosive player I've ever seen," says Blight. "And when you think about it an explosion is as good as it gets, as big as it gets. It's like a bomb going off, a shell from a cannon. He changed more games than any other player I've ever seen." Ablett's ability to do these things on both sides also used to please his coach. "That was something I probably prided myself on," says Blight. "He could kick it long right foot and very long left foot. I used to have a bit of fun with him at training, trying to match him with the left and right foot."

Blight had to fight Ablett to get him to play close to goal. "He felt he was a half-forward flanker. In '89 he'd mainly start wing, but then go to the forward pocket, because I didn't want to burn him out." Blight says that endurance running was one of the few chinks in Ablett's magical repertoire. "But he was a freak. I loved watching him play."

The margin is suddenly 17 points. The underdog is rising, and the needle on the stadium noise is moving into the red zone. Players hack the ball off the ground—Dear for Hawthorn, Steve Hocking for Geelong. It falls to Bos, in space, on the wing. He sees Ablett. Again, Ablett soars, but this time the pack is too big. While airborne, Langford nudges him forward with an elbow. The umpire probably misses a free kick.

It doesn't matter. Hamilton stays down, accepts the crumb, and squeezes it in for his second. We focus so much on Madigan's youth and inexperience, but Hamilton is the youngest man on the ground. He's only just turned 19 and is playing only his 13th game. It's his sixth appearance for the year. Four of them are finals. From the final round of the home and away season to this moment he's kicked 11 goals. He's also had a blinding game, and this is its exclamation point. It's a credit to Blight's coaching. In the last quarter he starts his half-forward flankers, Cameron and Hamilton, on the half-back line, issuing them the instruction to run through the centre in waves. It's an innovative tactic, and the Hawks half-backs are working overtime to spot them coming.

"I thought it actually hit the post," says Maginness. "I complained to the goal umpire that the ball hit the post." The goal umpire is not having it. He steps forward in the lab coat and neat, wide-brimmed hat and almost sticks Maginness with his emphatic, dual-finger salute. For the first time since the early stages of the game, the Cats are within two goals.

Bucketloads of time is left.

51

FINE PIECE OF MACHINERY

Gary Ayres is on the bench, his thigh muscle torn. But he's desperate to return to the field. Platten isn't yet at the hospital, but probably should be. He's sitting next to Ayres on the pine, still talking incessantly, unable to make sense of the game or his surrounds.

"Johnny didn't have any idea what was going on," says Ayres. "It was constantly 'How much in front are we?' I'd say, 'Five goals.' Then another goal. Johnny: 'How much in front are we?' Four goals. Another goal. Johnny: 'How much in front are we?'. 'Three goals'."

By the time it gets to two goals Ayres is awash with frustration and panic. "I keep saying (to runner George Stone), 'I'm ready to go, George, I'm ready to go!' And George is saying. 'Just stay there!' And the phone keeps ringing. So, I've got the phone ringing in one ear hoping to get back on, and I've got Johnny in the other ear asking how much in front are we. At two goals, I've just turned to Johnny and said, 'Johnny will you fucking shut up?' But he had no idea."

"We were on our knees," says Anderson. "I got a message halfway through the last quarter from Stoney, saying Tucky's split the webbing through his hand and I might have to tag Bairstow." A minute or two later Stone returns to Anderson. "Tucky's going to stay with Bairstow, you just keep running."

With nine minutes left and the Cats within 11 points, the team's best endurance runner does just that. Tuck tackles Bairstow yet again, grasping the man he's kept to just 12 disposals, refusing to let go despite his mangled hand. Dipper hacks the loose ball off the ground and Buckenara gathers in space at half-forward, draws a player, handballs over the top, and now it's just Anderson and the goals. He hunches his shoulders, steadies, and steers it through, dead centre. A paper volcano erupts out of the Hawthorn cheer squad. The lead is back to 17 points.

Anderson believes Tuck is the unheralded hero of his and Hawthorn's final goal. "I've coached a fair bit," says Anderson, "and when I talk to kids I talk about the importance of moments in games. The fact Tucky continued with his job, with his hand in a mess, he just had that single-minded focus to fulfil his role as captain. What it meant was that I could keep running, and we needed legs."

This is Tuck's 383rd game and he is 36 years old. He has six tackles for the day, more than any other man on the field. Watching replays now, it's the spidery-limbed Tuck, with the Jim's Mowing beard, who possesses the tackling technique and closing speed you'd most readily compare to the footballer of 2020. And in '89 he's not even close to the end. The next year he'll come second in the Peter Crimmins Medal as a 37-year-old, the seventh time he's runner-up. Two years later he'll lift the Cup again, in his 11th Grand Final, for his seventh and final premiership, in the last of his 426 games—a retirement he tries to avoid before the club overrules.

Tuck will be forced off the list in November 1991, at the age of 38, firmly of the belief he deserves another year. Given that I was added to the Hawthorn list that same day and stayed there for eight months, and managed zero games, he probably had a point, but at least it provided some symmetry in Wilson family history: as Tuck took his first steps into League football my father took his last—in 1972, the year I was born.

What a freak of nature was Michael Tuck. As Jeans so succinctly put it: "Michael Tuck, a fine piece of machinery."

52

NUMBER NINE

Having said all that, Tuck costs his team the next goal. With the pressure valves hissing, the ball is tapped in the skipper's direction by Dear. Rather than take possession, Tuck either hears a voice behind him, or attempts to find safety in the boundary to soak up more time. But he gets it horribly wrong. He knocks the ball over his head, hard and backwards towards the Geelong goal, into the hands of his direct opponent, Mark Bairstow. Bairstow is in space and running. He handballs and finds Bruns, who hoofs the ball high to the top of the square ...

Abbbbblettttt!

He does all the hard work while the ball is in flight. Ablett, in prime position, just nudges Langford forwards—a perfect use of hip and elbow—and from that moment it's always going to be his. He marks in front of his eyes, seven metres out, the angle a little tougher than 45 degrees. Today's footballer might run around. Ablett kicks the straightest of drop punts.

There's delirium now. Eleven points the difference. A window to the impossible has blown wide open and it's banging on its hinges. It's Ablett's ninth—equalling Gordon Coventry's 1928 Grand Final record, moving him past Brereton's eight in a losing team in '85. In the next 30 years, only Stephen Kernahan will come close with seven in a losing side against Essendon in 1993. The noise peaks as both sets of fans holler at their prize-fighters. The challenger is raining blows, the champ pushed back on the ropes, taking hits.

Gee-long! Clap, clap, clap. Gee-long! Clap, clap, clap.

"When they write the book on Grand Finals, this will rank with the best of them," surmises Dennis Cometti. It's better than that, Dennis—it gets its own book.

"I remember thinking, 'Shit, we're in a bit of strife here'," says Kennedy. "I'm thinking, we've got to hang on, you know, we've got to hang on. And I think we're all thinking that, and you're playing every moment—every moment you're playing it. You're trying to do everything you possibly can to hang on and hang on and hang on, because they were coming, and you could sense it. It's hard to stop. Momentum's an amazing thing—it's very hard to stop once it gets going, and they had it in the last quarter."

In the coach's box, Jeans is swamped with that sick sense of helplessness that goes with heavy investment and zero control. There is no television screen in the box and no countdown clock either. Jeans has two young statisticians keeping time. Chairman of selectors Brian Coleman remembers him barking: "How long to go?" "We reckon about five minutes," was the first response. As the Ablett show heads towards its finale, Jeans is beside himself. "How long to go! You said five minutes and it's been more than five minutes! How long? How long to go?' Coleman says the flustered young statisticians try to defend themselves. "They said, 'They keep kicking goals! It's going longer because they keep kicking goals!'"

With 2:30 left on the clock, Curran has a chance to finish it. He starts his approach where the boundary meets the 50-metre line at the city end, on the southern side of the ground, and streamers wind their way around his ankles. He takes his full 30 seconds and boos ring out. But Curran says he wasn't deliberately wasting time, just following his routine. He hits it well, but the kick misses. "I just pulled it," says Curran. "It missed by probably a foot to the left-hand side. But it made it (Hawthorn's lead) 12 points, so in some ways it changed the dynamic, because they'd have to score three times [to win], not twice. If something happened and they scored, we'd come back for a replay."

Something does happen and Geelong scores. After Hawthorn has spent the best part of 45 seconds winding down the clock, the move begins at half-back. Hovering at the edge of his defensive 50, Garry Hocking roves his brother's spoil of Curran and knows immediately that the open southern side is Geelong's best and possibly last chance, so he rolls the dice. His tired drop punt is wobbly and hangs awkwardly in the air, and Dipper seems poised to mark it and kill off the game, but Lindner lunges desperately, gets a fist in, and the ball is free. Now the Cats are out. Hamilton gathers—what a game the teenager has played—and pokes it forward to Scott, who has had a shocker but gathers the ball cleanly on Geelong's half-forward flank on the outer side. There is a saying in football: 'When it isn't your day, it can still be your moment' and Scott seems to heed it as he lowers his eyes and jets into the corridor. In front of him is David Cameron in acres of space, 30 metres from goal. When all around him have been run ragged, Scott calmly guides the ball onto his left foot for a neat pass to the unmarked Cameron, hitting him lace out.

The commentators start baying at Cameron: "He'll have to kick it quickly because there's under a minute left!" shrieks Ian Robertson. "Move it ... Panic stations!" "He's taking too long!" bellows Don Scott.

Cameron himself is a picture of calm. He's 25 years old and playing his 35th game, and with his skinny arms and shiny blond hair, complete with Ricky Schroder ear flaps, he's hardly the archetype of a football hero. But as the stadium immolates around him, he stands still at the top of his approach. His grip on the ball seems light, his shoulders relaxed. He takes a deliberate breath, walks a little, eyes on the target, then some tiny steps, and then a gentle acceleration. In the kicking stride, his eyes lower and his left arm extends, and he guides the ball so precisely. He makes sweet contact and the goal umpire doesn't move. I time it as 20 seconds exactly from mark to goal. It's one of the best and most technically perfect set shots I've ever seen.

Cameron didn't take too long. He kicked the goal, and he gave his team a final shot.

Six points now separate Hawthorn and Geelong. There are 38 seconds on the clock.

53

THE SIREN

Robert DiPierdomenico isn't the only hero of the two centre bounces that finish the game. Greg Dear wins the first tap, his longshanks looking even longer in this era of brief shorts. He's rucked alone all day, four exhausting quarters, and although Flanigan had the better of the last three, in 1989 Dear is Hawthorn's most underrated and indispensable player. He receives 11 votes in the Brownlow that year; in a team full of stars only Platten and Dunstall poll more votes.

Bews is superb too. He roves the ball perfectly at both bounces and has two frantic attempts at last clearance nirvana. Ultimately, the desperation of the opposition and sheer weight of numbers close him down. I feel his game is grossly underrated, possibly because Don Scott pillories him all day from the commentary box. He has 27 disposals, more than anyone else on the ground—seven more than Pritchard and Buckenara, who have the most for the Hawks. He fights to the bitter end. When I ask him for an interview for this book, he just sighs: "Do I really have to talk about it? Again?"

Curran deserves acknowledgement too. With the floating bone in his knee hampering his running, he charges off the line at centre half-forward. As Bews gathers, pirouettes, and is poised to handball, Curran lunges, and a flailing limb prevents the ball reaching its target. Then the ball squirms loose and Curran claims Couch in a follow-up tackle. The seconds tick. The rucks battle again, and this time it's Curran, together with DiPierdomenico, who sandwiches Bews. Then Dipper collapses on the ball. And that's it.

"Somebody blew the bloody siren," says Blight on *The Final Story* documentary. "One. Bloody. Kick."

It seems almost inconceivable to those of us looking on, but while the game was still going, a lot of players made a point of not looking at the scoreboard and didn't realise how narrow Hawthorn's escape was. Wittman knew it was close but not that close. Says Madigan: "I never looked at the scoreboard when I was playing ... I didn't have any inclination the score had got so close ... I thought we were six goals or so up or something ... when I looked up at the end I thought, 'Shit, that was pretty close'."

When Flanigan looked up he just thought, "shit".

"We really only got to within two goals with two or three minutes to go," he says. "Every time we got close, they'd kick one, so you can't really look at the scoreboard. You just look at the next contest, next contest, next contest. And then at the end of the game you look up and go, 'Hmmm, that's not good'."

Lindner knew the score. For the final seconds he'd pushed forward, and says he was out and clear if Bews had miraculously squeezed it to the outside. "I'd left my opponent," says Lindner. "I figured you might as well lose by two and give yourself a chance at the draw." He then grins sadly. "What if he got one of those toe pokes out? Maybe I kick a goal and we draw the game? Or maybe I kick a point and we lose by five."

"Relief," says Curran—the word every single Hawthorn player chooses. Relief.

Jeans is now at ground level, and hugs his injured champion, Ayres—the man he convinced not to move to Glenorchy all those years ago. "We only just got it done," says Kennedy. "But we got it done. If it goes for another five minutes, I don't think we win the game."

Maginness shakes Brownless's hand and runs to his teammates. "It was just sheer bliss when that siren went—we'd actually done it, achieved it. It was a feeling that I've never actually experienced ever before. That sense of relief and jubilation and I suppose solidarity within the group."

"A massive emptiness," was what Flanigan was feeling. He walks from the centre square, biting his mouthguard, trying to hold it together. At three o'clock the next morning he'll be propped against the bar at the Valley Inn with his coach, and Blight will say: "Darren, I didn't think you could play that well." Flanigan responds with a laugh: "Thanks for the vote of confidence, coach!"

"I had three in-depth conversations with Blighty in three years," Flanigan says, "and that was one of them."

As Hawthorn players confront the scale of their achievement, Channel Seven boundary rider Michael Roberts runs to Jeans and asks: "What's it like to have back-to-back premierships?" This quest has been his life, his driving obsession for 12 months, but Jeans gives Roberts nothing. "Great, great," the coach says, and his eyes brim with tears, and then he spurns the microphone in favour of hugging Buckenara. It's left to Buckenara to provide the audio content: "We won it for Jeansy, Joycey, and all the boys who couldn't make it."

As the Hawthorn players embrace, the losers' world closes in. Says Flanigan: "A lot of players and staff were distraught, and that sort of tears at your heart." Dipper falls into a bear hug with Bews. "Sorry mate. There can only be one winner," he says.

Blight thinks that every year the loser gets unfairly lost in our Grand Finals: "I've said this for years, I've said it before I coached Geelong: the runners-up in a lot of sports get a medal. Now, if it wasn't for Peter Moore throwing his away (in 1981; a gesture which prompted the

League to discontinue presenting medals for runners-up), I reckon the other side should get acknowledged and I felt that as a player too ... The fact you were there. The fact you were a part of it. I think that gets downplayed and the fault lies with the people in the media."

Blight likes a South Australian footy tradition. "In the week after the game, the two teams go to the West End Brewery in Hindmarsh. And there's a ceremonial painting of the chimney. The top six feet are the colours of the club that won, underneath at three feet is the other team, half the size, but both teams go there and celebrate the game ...I've always said I love it. You acknowledge both teams."

On this famous Saturday, in the spring twilight, the only spoils go to the winners. Bulldogs Legend Ted Whitten leans into the microphone: "It's my pleasure to present this premiership cup to Hawthorn's captain Michael Tuck, and their coach Allan Jeans."

The cup is raised. No confetti cannons. No teammates swamping the podium. Just a smile and a handshake between captain and coach as they each hold a handle, savouring the delivery on a promise, waving to the crowd.

Platten is there in all the footage and photos, grinning proudly. "The blokes carried me on Dunstall's shoulders, I cannot remember anything of it," he says. He'll be taken to hospital soon enough. At 11pm he'll get up in an attempt to join the celebrations, take one step, vomit, and return to his hospital bed. "It's pretty sad," says Platten. "Of all of my footy career, all the games I played, and I played 371 League games all up ... That'd be the one game I wish I'd finished up playing. It's a bit sad."

Brereton gets to the finish line, sore and bleeding, but unbowed. When I ask him about the post-game festivities, he gets a little wistful and talks about the light: "It's funny though, there's always the same light, because it finishes later, that gets cast over the ground at the final siren. Seven other times at the final siren on Grand Final day, the light is very long coming over that Southern Stand, and yeah, it feels like Spring— it's not just the end of the game, it's the end of that year.

It signifies the end of every pace you've taken since last October."

It's true. If I'm honest, I've put that paragraph in just to annoy fans of other clubs. Whereas you may think of the smell of pollen or the swooping of magpies, when Dermott Brereton ponders the changing of the seasons, he pictures the light from the centre of the MCG on Grand Final day.

54

THE THING ABOUT DIPPER

DiPierdomenico doesn't make it to the presentation ceremony. Ted Whitten shakes his hand as the two cross paths, but now Dipper's burly chest is inflating, and his lungs are audibly hissing.

An ambulance is waiting at the door to the rooms.

I ask all the players for their defining moment of the 1989 Grand Final. There are so many to choose from—classic screamers, long goals, extraordinary courage, precision kicking, random violence, plotted violence, Yeates and Brereton, Ablett, Ablett and more Ablett.

The answer from Chris Langford is my favourite. He delivered it in a small, formal meeting room on Level 18 of a South Yarra office block. Thirty years on from the most famous game of his career, Langford is as fit as ever but has some silvery hair now to accompany that lantern jaw and the model looks. Around him there are ornamental copies of *The Great Gatsby* and *Catcher in the Rye* doing the job of corporate decorating. The view across towards Yarra Park is arresting. It feels, in other words, as far from the MCG as it's possible to be while still being able to see it. At the very end of our interview, Langford takes me back there:

"The moment I remember was when they were eleven points down, and the ball was contested and came loose from a marking contest. It came loose pretty much on the edge of the square, on their half-forward flank on the Southern Stand side. It was maybe a couple of minutes to go on the clock, they were coming home with a wet sail, it was down to the wire, and there were four pairs of Geelong and Hawthorn players, one on one, and the ball is in the middle.

"Eight people almost in a circle, *Ring-a-Ring-a-Rosie*. The ball's in the middle. And it's that whole thing: 'Do I leave my man?' Ablett's there, do I go, or is he peeling off to try and get a handball? What do I do? And Buddha Hocking is there, and Neville Bruns is there, these guys loitering, and then Dipper dives on the ball. It was just that moment of hesitation when everyone is going, "What do I do, do I peel off? Or do I go for it, do I peel off?"

Dipper's jumped on it.

We didn't know Dipper's state of health, his state of repair at that time. We had no idea. But at that point I knew we've got 'em...Always believed we had them, and then I begin to have doubts as they kicked a few goals, those last two or three, I'm thinking, 'Maybe we are down and out here, we're on the ropes,' and then that contest when Dipper dived on the ball, and everyone's then jumped on top of him and the umpire called ball up, I thought, 'That's it. That's it. We want this more than they do.' The fact Dipper did it with broken ribs is ridiculous.

That's it for me, that's my favourite Dipper story. He was fearless, he was tough—not tough as in go out and hurting people, and yes, he did that, he did hurt people—but he was tough because you couldn't hurt him. He was tough because he didn't feel it and didn't worry about it. So yeah, a lot of people say he was tough because he had sharp elbows and this sort of thing. Dipper was tough because you could beat it up, you could break it, you could cut it, it didn't make any difference, you didn't stop Dipper that way. The only way you could stop Dipper was get the ball, run faster, jump higher—you couldn't beat Dipper mentally or physically, you had to beat him with skill.

And there aren't many footballers like that. There are guys who can run back and take a mark looking at the ball and all that sort of stuff, but they're still skin and bones, they're still flesh, and they still feel pain and they still get knocked about and they still get hurt. But Dipper wasn't like that. It wasn't that he did spectacular, courageous things running back with the flight of the ball, it was the fact that you couldn't hurt him. He was just so physically tough. And mentally tough. And I don't think there are many people you can honestly describe as that type of footballer, that were just good and fearless and unbreakable.

When it comes to my moment of that Grand Final, nothing comes close to that… Dipper played most of the game with broken ribs and a punctured lung and was still the one who made the difference at the end."

55

PAIN AND EXHAUSTION

Four-goal hero Dean Anderson says that after relief, the next thing to hit him was exhaustion. "I remember after that game, sitting in the rooms with extreme stomach pain, and that would have lasted two or three hours. That night I enjoyed going out, but I was done by about 11pm. I just went back and saw some mates and went to bed. I was probably in bed by 12. Just nothing left."

Brereton, with his damaged kidney, was given the directive to stay off the alcohol. "I was told to definitely under no circumstances have anything to drink that day. I think I ended up figuring that day finished at midnight, so from 12.01am, I might have sneaked one or two."

Sunday Age reporter Steve Perkin had the job of assisting with Brereton's weekly newspaper column for the next morning's paper. "Normally he would handwrite them and deliver them during the week," Perkin says. "But that obviously wasn't going to work, so the idea was that I'd go into the rooms and put a tape recorder on him."

It was noisy amid the celebrations, so Brereton led Perkin into the shower area. "I remember he sat down on the edge of a large bathtub (yes, the same bath!), and I gave him my tape recorder. My first question was, 'Tell me what happened in the opening few minutes'."

So, Brereton starts the story, the first telling before a lifetime of retellings. "And in talking about it he stopped at one point," says Perkin, "and spat into the bath, and it was all blood. I looked at him and said, 'Have you taken a head knock as well?' And he said, 'No I'm bleeding internally.' And then he told me, 'I was bleeding internally at half-time. The doctors saw it and wanted me to come off, but I said, 'No, this is a Grand Final, there's no way I'm coming off.' So, he played out the game with the knowledge that somewhere inside he was bleeding."

It all feeds a story that makes Brereton one of the most compelling footy figures of his time. The next season he'll play with injured ribs, wear an inflatable vest under his jumper and kick a career-best 11 goals against Richmond. In 1991 he'll win his fifth and final premiership in a Hawthorn team written off as too old and too slow. He's only just turned 27 at that point but his body is battered worse than a man who has played League football for twice as long, and his salad days are over—he'll play just six more games for the Hawks, followed by strange, mostly forgotten seasons for Sydney (1994) and Collingwood (1995). But at the end of his storied career it's this day—the 1989 Grand Final—that is placed above all others.

Says Brereton: "By and large I got marked as a sporting person and an individual that day. Had I not been smacked around and had not been able to get up, I would have been marked differently in my life. So that has a major and profound effect on my life and the psyche of my life, and the knowledge of what I can and can't be." The Yeates-Brereton saga, a three-act revenge drama played out in footy boots, even has a coda during the end-of-season international exhibition tour. "We were in London and we went to the pub," says Yeates. "I'd had plenty and Dermie was in the pub. I went over to him, stupidly, and stuck my hand out, and was about to say, 'Bygones be bygones, and all the best,' but he didn't want to shake my hand, which is fair enough.

I didn't shake his hand earlier in the year."

The situation then escalated. "I thought, 'Hello, it's on here'," recalls Yeates. In the end, teammates intervened. "I think Piggy Dunstall and Dwayne Russell and others stepped in and ushered me away," says Yeates. "But yeah, obviously he was upset … Don't know why…"

Yeates says before the Grand Final he had planned to retire, and that he and Mark Bos had made a pact: "I would have been out. But because of what happened with Dermott, there was no way known I was going to retire. It's not the done thing. To hit then piss off. I wanted to give him another crack."

The two played on each other in round one of 1990. "It was a sad occasion actually," remembers Yeates. "I'd just lost my brother two weeks prior to the game." Blight tried to convince Yeates to miss the game. "I said, 'You've gotta be jokin', right?'" says Yeates. Then Blight named another defender to man Brereton. Yeates just walked over at the bounce and changed the match-up. "They thumped us that day," says Yeates. "But out of the contest between me and Dermott, I think maybe I had the better of him."

The stats say Brereton kicked five goals from 20 possessions. Yeates had nine kicks and a handball. Memories can get a little clouded. Hawthorn won by 115 points. There endeth the saga.

Today the two of them play off each other like old friends, almost with a sense of vaudeville. Writer John Harms tells of a Geelong lunch he attended at The Sofitel hotel, where Yeates and Brereton re-enacted the whole thing in pretend slow-motion. "Seven hundred Geelong fans were cheering as Dermott lay flat on his back, stamping his foot," grins Harms. "It was great theatre."

"He's a ripper bloke," says Brereton of Yeates. "A good fella." Says Yeates of Brereton: "He came down when Bluey McGrath had his cancer scare and he helped raise a lot of money for Bluey. We paid him with a bottle of wine. I've got that much respect for him."

56

NOT FAR AWAY

"The game was Ablett's in the same way as magic was Merlin's." Martin Flanagan wrote that line for *The Age* about Ablett's 1989 preliminary final, but it's just as true of Grand Final day. And as completely as he dominated footy's grandest stage, he shrank from its aftermath. He sat in the change rooms, peeling off socks and strapping, his expression matching the tenor of the room, which is the muted murmur of defeat. Reporters descended en masse, all trying to fathom the unfathomable. How did he do it? How did an individual performance like that happen?

"It's a team game," Ablett muttered. "Individualism is irrelevant … we came back well as a team … I think we can hold our heads high … as I said, it's a team game."

Later, after Ablett had showered, *Sunday Age* journalist Caroline Wilson approached the Geelong champion. Ablett was wearing only a towel. Wilson was 29 years old and five months pregnant, and with her terrier style, had been investigating and writing a warts-and-all profile of Ablett for her paper. It was ready to run the next morning and it was timed perfectly—even without his virtuoso performance as a prompter, the country had never been hungrier for Ablett stories—but she needed to ask him one question, so that the man may rebut certain rumours that had entered the public domain: had Ablett ever been to jail?

Ablett smiled. "You're having another go, are you?"

"I realise it's not the best time," replied Wilson. "But it might be hard to catch up with you later on."

What happened next was nothing short of strange. Ablett noticed that Wilson was pregnant and placed a hand on her belly. "He looked down and smiled beatifically," says Wilson. "Almost like he was blessing the baby." Where most reporters would have been thrown, she repeated her question, and said that the piece would explore his past, the bad as well as the good, that it would refer to his somewhat wild youth, the odd court appearance. She said she'd checked and double-checked her sources and that, overall, felt it was an honest and fair portrayal.

"There wouldn't be anything bad to write about would there?" replied Ablett. Then, with a wink, he walked away.

Wilson says the mood in the rooms wasn't as despondent as some she's seen after Grand Final defeats. "There was a sense that they'd done their best, that they'd thrown everything at Hawthorn and just come up short," she says. "I think there was real pride in the performance and also maybe a sense that they'd been involved in something special. I remember speaking to Damian Bourke and he said, 'They're the benchmark,' which sounds like a trite phrase, but the way he said it, there was just so much respect. I still remember it."

There was also a sense the Cats were a young side on the cusp of their own golden era. Everyone felt it. When the team was received at the Geelong Town Hall later that night, it was not a scene of jubilation, but there was no pall of despair. Good times were surely coming. As Rohan Connolly enthused in his Monday match report for *The Age*: "Unlike other newcomers to the big day who have been taught through humiliation just what is required to win them, Geelong caught on so quickly that it went from the receiving end of a hiding to almost pinching a premiership. Few losing Grand Finallists have been able to face the next season with as much optimism as the Cats will enter 1990."

Blight sensed it too. He remembers having what he calls a "melancholy moment" in the coach's box, about halfway through the last quarter, with the team four or five goals down. "I remember having a conversation with Bruce Nankervis, and I said, 'We're not far away here …' I dunno if this is a good thing or a bad thing to say, but I said, 'We're not far away. We just need another one or two players … another couple of players.' Mind you, then we started to get closer and it was, 'Ooh, hang on a second here…'"

With 30 years' hindsight, Blight says what was missing was a great defender. "That was always the problem with Geelong. I just couldn't get that one great defender. Every premiership team for 100 years has had one great defender, and if you have two you usually win multiple flags. You look at Mew, Langford, Ayres. You look at Hawthorn recently. We just couldn't find that one great defender at Geelong. We had some handy players, but not great."

One of those "handy players", Tim Darcy, pretty much agrees. "We were pretty small," he says. "Michael Schulze and I were the key defenders. I'm only six two and Mick would have probably been six three. Later on, Tim McGrath, he wasn't much taller. We were always a bit light on in terms of size … I was recruited as a forward and ended up going back …maybe the best of a bad bunch, I dunno. We were certainly small to play those key roles."

57

THE REASON

Malcolm Blight didn't re-watch the game for ten years. Then one night, in 1999, after his time at Adelaide had come to an end, he was at a friend's house in Melbourne and it popped up on *Fox Footy*, and he just started watching the game, the viewing of which has been an annual ritual for so many of us. Blight found himself making it all the way to the end.

"That first quarter, it was the kicking of Hawthorn that absolutely split us open," Blights exclaims. "They didn't miss! I hadn't seen it matched until the 2007 game when Geelong split Port Adelaide open. The kicking! Blokes not even changing gears. It had nothing to do with people running into each other. So that just reminded me of why they won multiple premierships. They were the best kicking side by far. That's what split us—not all the other stuff. They were just too good with their kicking in that first part. They didn't miss!"

What Blight means by "the other stuff" is the well-ventilated theory that Geelong lost the game in the first quarter because its focus was the man and not the ball. It's not a fringe view. In fact, Blight's own players fan these flames:

Mark Bairstow: "The thing I don't understand ... we played with attacking flair all year ... and then in the Grand Final (Blight) made a lot of changes in the biggest game of the year. In my opinion, I thought we made mistakes, worrying about knocking bloody Brereton over, worrying about players playing in different areas. Let them worry about us and let us go! We might've been down, but we wouldn't have been 40 points down ..."

Bairstow again: "To turn around in the Grand Final and to basically try to be the aggressor not so much at the ball, but at the man? I thought it cost us early, and it cost us badly."

Paul Couch, on *Open Mike*: "We went the knuckle too early."

Darren Flanigan: "We gave away a lot of silly free kicks. Trying to be a little over-aggressive as a group."

Bruce Lindner: "We hadn't played that way. I can't remember any lead-up games where there was an elbow here and a serious off the ball incident somewhere else. Our lead-up games were hard good footy."

The Hawks players reinforce it, too.

Scott Maginness: "I think they were focused more on the man."

Dean Anderson: "They were late with tackles, late with hits. It was a physical game."

Peter Curran: "Their approach was essentially to try and brutalise us. I think it played into our hands, because if they hadn't done that, we would have been forced to defend against them ... They went us, and we went whack, whack, whack on the scoreboard."

Greg Madigan: "I was thinking to myself: 'They're playing themselves out of the game!' (Garry) Hocking and Bews and these guys are just continually giving away penalties! I'm thinking, 'This is great!'"

In his wonderful and cathartic chapter on the 1989 Grand Final in *Loose Men Everywhere* (Text Publishing, 2002), sportswriter and Geelong tragic John Harms puts it as starkly as this: "... in this drama ... Hawthorn is the hero, Geelong is the villain. Good has triumphed.

And the villain has learnt a moral lesson. I am glad Hawthorn won."

It's hard for outsiders to say if Geelong was affected by the Yeates-Brereton sub-plot. I do have some sympathy for Blight, though. I was there at Waverley to see Brereton destroy Essendon in that second semi-final and was just 20 rows away when he turned the lights out on Vander Haar and the Bombers. I heard the sickening contact. It was High Noon stuff. Then he took out two more. Was Blight meant to cross his fingers and hope for the best? He chose to do something and to do it within the very rules that Brereton had been exploiting. And it almost worked.

Did it give his players bloodlust? Did they lose focus on the footy? The comments by the Geelong players suggest it may have, although I'm not so sure whether those views are informed, more than anything else, by the result. It's easy for errors to be magnified by the harsh lens of defeat. There were 18 Geelong players on that field, and most were fighting for the ball. After the opening bounce Yeates gave away only one free kick—a follow-up shot at Brereton, off the ball—but a conclusion we could reach is that only one player lost control, and it's the same player who lost his teeth: Garry Hocking.

Re-watch the game: it's Buddha landing punches on Dipper. It's Buddha who leaps late into Kennedy and Dipper giving away two goals.

It's Buddha who hits Platten often enough that nobody's sure which is the concussion blow. Yes, there's some pushing and shoving, and a fairly scary constrictor hold by Bews, but Hawthorn is up to its neck in that stuff too.

Jeans often gets the credit for his team's ball focus. Coleman says that at the time Brereton went down, Jeans was on his feet in the box yelling, "Don't try to get square now, let's get goals in front! Play footy! Play footy!" Madigan remembers the same message on the bench: 'Play the ball, play the ball and everything will happen around it!'

And yet, on this famous and dangerous day, the one Blight calls "the last of the truly brutal Grand Finals", the violence flowed both ways.

Remember Ayres lining up Ablett in the first ten minutes, Brereton flying in at Darcy, all knees and legs, Buckenara's crude and high tackle on Hocking, Curran going late and high on Lindner, Brereton squeezing Steve Hocking behind the windpipe. After quarter-time, Brereton also had his own crack at Yeates, payback on the payback, there's Ayres bumping Couch late and high, and, of course, Dipper elbowing Garry Hocking to the mouth—as bad as anything you'll see. He was lucky he only got five matches.

What the Hawks managed expertly was fierce concentration on the ball, but with an eye to violence when the moment presented. They didn't get distracted by the Brereton hit. They reached a divine equipoise between hurting the Cats on the scoreboard and hurting them in the contest. They were that sort of team—skillful and frightening. Not many teams are like that, so ruthless and so brilliant at the same time. Perhaps only Brisbane's sides of 2001-03 compare, coached as they were by Leigh Matthews, a man steeped in the Hawthorn way. It's why this back-to-back Hawthorn team of 1988-89 is one of the greatest of all time.

Indeed, rather than saying Geelong's early tactics cost them the game, it might just be that the opposite is true: that the hits in the first quarter nearly *won* the Cats the game. Brereton, although inspirational, had nine disposals for the day. In the second half especially, he played like a man in pain. Then there was Platten. In 1989, he was the best rover in the League. Buddha whacked him out of the game—just three kicks for the day from the most talented small man on the ground. What was that worth to Geelong's fortunes? As for Dipper, he was best on ground when Ablett collected him. He stayed on and played well, but surely at a reduced output. And with Platten benched, injured players remained on the ground. There's a cost to that, too.

Blight might have a point. Maybe the quarter-time margin wasn't about ball focus or otherwise, but pure football ability? By that analysis, Geelong's tactics nearly snatch it.

Dunstall expressed the conundrum in *Inside the Battle of '89*: "In the first quarter, we really concentrated on the ball as much as we could, we kicked as many goals as we could and we built up a very good lead … whether you'd say it was a bad tactic (by Geelong) I don't know, because as time was running out at the end, they just about brought it back to all square. So, the tactic I guess in a sense worked for them, but it may also have cost them the game."

I ask Blight if he'd change anything about how his team approached the game. "Maybe not (do) the Brereton bit," he says, sighing. "I still trust my instinct about what was going to happen. Dermott, I've spoken to him about it. He says no he wasn't, but he was coming, you know. Couchy wasn't very far away from him. And now I don't disbelieve him, but I still think he mightn't have thought it but he would have done it. Because that's what he does."

Damian Drum, a future coach of Fremantle (1999-2001) is a staunch defender of Blight, his great mentor. Drums says: "He [Brereton] was making an absolute beeline for Couch. Why do you think he doesn't see Yeatesy coming? He doesn't see him because he has his eyes locked purely on Couch. It was a good call from Blight. It was a courageous effort from Brereton, but in those days it was legal—Malcolm was absolutely right to use the tactic."

58

MORE REASONS

One other advantage Hawthorn enjoyed during the 1989 Grand Final, often overlooked in analyses of the game, was the week of rest it had as Geelong slugged it out in the preliminary final. Nowadays there's much ink spilled in Grand final week as analysts ponder six-day breaks versus seven-day breaks. In 1989 the winner of the second semi-final earned a 14-day break. On a warm, humid, September day, fresh legs probably helped.

Then there's the experience factor. In Hawthorn's team, just three players—Madigan, Condon, and Anderson—were making their Grand Final debuts. Four—Dunstall, Dear, Curran and Platten—were playing their fourth, Buckenara and Langford their fifth. Kennedy was in his sixth. Mew, Ayres and Brereton were playing their seventh, Dipper his eighth. And Tuck, unbelievably, was playing his tenth.

At Geelong, all 20 men were playing their *first* Grand Final.

Experience was an asset on so many levels. Consider the navigation of Grand Final week: the increased media; the crowds at training; the Grand Final parade; sleeping the night before; the arrangement of tickets for family and friends. Everything was easier for having done it before. "We'd done it so many times," says Kennedy of the Grand Final week rigmarole. "It was almost like shelling peas."

Langford talks about his inner calm when he was running onto the ground. "When you run out, by the time I'd played in a couple of Grand Finals ... We were pretty good at being focused and well readied and not too over the top. You're not there looking around in awe, you're not there with your ears glued to the crowd and everything that's going on. You are absolutely in your own head, and to me it's like, you can hear this dull noise in the background, and you're not really taking notice of it."

During the pre-game period, Collins, who'd played in two Grand Finals already, took Madigan down the race to sit on the bench, and they sat together. "Take it in now," Collins said to the teenager. "Drink it in and you'll be more used to it when it's for real." Anderson remembers benefitting from similar acts of leadership: "I had a lot of advice from players around what to expect—people like Tucky and Ayrsey."

Wittman recalls Jeans's Grand Final week mantra about it being just another game. "You almost have to trick your brain," Wittman says. "You've got to trigger it to the point where it thinks it's just another game ... and that keeps you under control and from burning too much energy and adrenaline before the game actually starts. So, the experience of blokes playing year after year, that's massive in the end ... Because the guys have got so much experience just to get an extra half hour's sleep, to relax in the morning, to maybe have a stretch, to have the same breakfast. If you overthink it, and overthink the prize, and overthink what you're trying to do, you're going to blow it. You're going to cook yourself before the game starts."

And when fists start flying, and the elbows and forearms, experience helps with maintaining focus. This is what they do. Don't get carried away. Don't get sucked in. Play the ball.

In Stephen Phillips's documentary, *Inside The Battle of '89*, Jeans was asked his opinion on why his team won. He said: 'If you analyse the stats, the scores were close—there were only six points to separate us. The kicks, marks, handballs were close—there was not much to separate us there. But there was one significant difference: the media recorded us having 47 tackles to their 25. That was the point we were trying to get across, that's what we focused upon, and I believe that was the thing that broke their game down."

That was the decisive factor for the coach: Operation Tackle was mission accomplished.

As for other decisive factors, I always think that, in the close ones, luck plays a part. Luck with injuries (both sides suffered them), luck with the timing of momentum swings, sometimes just luck with the bounce of the ball. This was a Grand Final with 42 goals and 72 scoring shots, and the final margin was six points. That leads to an endless spiral of what- ifs. What if Flanigan's shot doesn't hit the post in the second quarter? What if he gets the 50-metre penalty he probably deserves? What if Scott kicks his easy shot in the last few minutes? What if Anderson's fluky left footer floats out of bounds on the full? Blight's haunted by Lindner playing on and Brereton's second mark. There are dozens more, and just as many slanted the other way. With a one-kick result, with 40 players and thousands of variables, you can chase these threads around forever. Who'd be a coach? How do you un-pick something so nuanced and multi-factorial?

And then there's the most obvious reason of all, the one hit on by Damian Bourke: Hawthorn was just better.

History backs up Bourke's assessment—not just because Hawthorn won the tightest and toughest Grand Final of the decade, although that has a huge impact. There's also the back-to-back flags; the fact the Hawks suffered only six losses across two seasons; there's the seven Grand Finals in a row; there are the all-time-greats on every line, especially the defence, where Blight correctly identifies a gap between the two sides. On all sorts of telling career metrics—games played, State selection honours, Brownlow votes, media awards—Hawthorn's team edges Geelong's. Of the nine '89 Grand Final players to be inducted as members of the Australian Football Hall of Fame so far, Hawthorn has seven (Ayres, Brereton, DiPierdomenico, Dunstall, Langford, Platten and Tuck) and Geelong just two (Ablett and Garry Hocking).

On this day, like in most Grand Finals, the better team did win. As Flanigan says: "They had a superstar team. If you look back in history at the number of absolute champions they had in their team, it would have been almost a bit of a travesty for us to pinch it in the end. Just because of how they played, and the depth of quality in their team."

59

HIGH ART

Malcolm Blight and his Geelong players might not agree with this, but to some extent the 1989 Grand Final transcends the concept of winners and losers. It's watched and re-watched by Hawthorn fans, obviously, but it's also watched religiously by Geelong fans too, and supporters of other clubs, as a symbol of what the game can be, or maybe just what it was—its peak.

"I call it the Woodstock of all Grand finals," says Wittman, "It's one of those things that over time becomes greater and bigger than life. To have played in the Woodstock of Grand Finals, I just feel so blessed."

Says Brereton: "Who knows what it was like to play in the Bloodbath Grand Final in the '40s, the iconic Grand Finals that people write about, but since television, that '89 Grand Final is probably numero uno, just for everything the game can offer. So, to play in that is a very fortunate thing to look back on."

Why do people love this game so much? For me, I get a real sense of nostalgia during my regular re-visits, not just for the players and the action, which I know almost play-by-play, but also for little accoutrements of the era—tight shorts, mullet haircuts, perms, the old MCG stands, terry-towelling dressing gowns, streamers, floggers, field umpires dressed in white, goal umpires in hats and coats, and a clean red footy free of sponsor's logos.

Footy had been on television for a while, but it's from about this point that coverage rapidly improves. There are enough cameras to satisfy the modern eye and the commentators are one of history's A-Teams: Dennis Cometti, destined for greatness, providing the bass notes and the gravitas; Ian Robertson, excitable, rapid-fire, knowledgeable and nasal; Don Scott, curmudgeonly and quotable on special comments (my friends and I still pepper our banter with some of his admonishments: "Pressure, Ian, pressure!" and "When are they going to learn that the pressure goes up in Grand Finals!") There's no cosying up to the players with Don. His eyes are peeled constantly for even a hint of fear.

But mostly it's the game, the game that's filled this book, this thrilling contest between two brilliant attacking teams.

Having engineered half of it, Malcolm Blight is as eloquent on the game's legacy as anyone: "It epitomised great skill. I mean there's a lot of goals kicked. And it was also brutal ... and brutal is a word you don't use very often ... It brought that to a new pinnacle. I hadn't seen a game as hard as that. I forgot how hard it was ... I think we had six blokes in hospital or doctored and they had six the same. It was probably the most physical game I've ever seen in 50 years of watching the game and it happened on that one day—all these physical acts happen, tied with the unbelievable brilliance of players and goals. That's what the game was all about."

I wonder how deliberately Blight chooses the word "was". Certainly, it's impossible to imagine this rate of scoring in the modern game. Forty- two goals between the teams, raining down at an average of one every two and a half minutes. And it's even more incomprehensible to the modern footy watcher when you consider the behinds, too. Very few of them were scrambled, rushed behinds, and so the exhilarating reality was something close to 72 shots at goal in 120 minutes. That's a score every minute and forty seconds. Ridiculous.

Blight calls it brutal. Langford calls it violent: "It was probably the last of the violent Grand Finals. I think people do like the violence part of it, the fact that Yeates cleaned up Dermott, Dipper got cleaned up by Ablett, Platts got concussed and had no idea what day it was. People like that. The fact there was that physical violence about it, it was around about that time trial by video started coming in."

This is undoubtedly true. What's also true is that football is now better for having eliminated much of its violence. Think of John Platten, punch drunk in his yellow dressing gown, having sustained the next in a series of head injuries that will eliminate his memory of the day, and affect his mental capacity for the rest of his life. The AFL had to act. Rules protecting the head and limiting shirtfronts were inevitable. As professionalism increased, the workplace had to be made as safe as possible. But that isn't to say that violence isn't compelling. We loved it. Blood and fear. Pain and vengeance. There's no legend of the 1989 Grand Final without violence. Every time I put on my old DVD of the game, the pre-roll starts, and I think: "This really shouldn't be rated G.' It's got Catwoman, Dipper and Garry Hocking. It's at least PG."

If you were billing it as a blockbuster film, it has everything. It has the big, colourful personalities. It has heroes to cheer and villains to boo. For the Hawks, Dermott, Dunstall, Dipper, Ayres, Platten, Buckenara, Langford and Tuck. For the Cats, Buddha, Lindner, Couch, Stoneham, Brownless, Bews and of course, most compelling of all, the man with the wispy hair wearing number five.

People love the game just because of Ablett. It's such a fast contest, and with so many individual acts of skill, but Ablett's freakishness sits beyond them all. Langford explains it perfectly: he didn't do what you expected a footballer to do, and he'd still pull it off. If they ever rate the Norm Smith of Norm Smiths, surely this is the one.

Says Flanigan: "There were a lot of personalities playing footy at that time, and both teams had personalities in them. I think it was pure footy. You played man-on-man, there weren't floods, there weren't presses, there was always six in the front half and six in the back half at every centre bounce, and it was still a really physical game. But the skill level … if you look at some of the games back in the seventies when the skill level wasn't so great … the skill of the players across the park was really high, so you had the unique combination of personalities of importance, of high scoring and in a brutal game of footy. And it was just a great event to be a part of."

Peter Schwab puts it like this: "The game wouldn't be played like that now. It just can't be. It's just not where it's at. It's gone past that. They're trying to change the game to open it up more, but that's always hard because there was no team defence back then. There was no zoning. There wasn't a lot of third man in. And there wasn't a lot of covering for each other or handing over. And there was nowhere near the constant physical pressure. There was pressure, and it was physical, but it wasn't constant like it is today. So, players now are constantly in and around traffic and if they beat one tackle, they've got another one coming. In our day, if you got through a tackle, you're probably out."

Says Curran: "I think just because it has so much drama to it, in some ways it's high art, it's theatre. You don't know the outcome, it's in the balance. There's conflict, there's acts of bravery, acts of courage. It has all the things that we admire about the game, and the pace and skill of the game in a lot of ways still holds up today. Obviously, the defensive mechanisms wouldn't allow it to happen, but the pace and the skill and the intensity of it, I think when you watch it, it still holds up."

60

A BEAUTIFUL ANACHRONISM

The 1989 Grand Final took place on the cusp of an era. The strength, skills, stamina, and professionalism of players had improved rapidly, which meant a jump in standard from what I think of as "black and white" footy. Looking back at the highlight reels, I enjoy the toughness of sixties and seventies games, and the genius of individuals like Bernie Quinlan, Darrel Baldock, Barry Cable, Leigh Matthews, Jezza and Blight. But play doesn't flow like Hawthorn and Geelong in '89. Players don't hit pinpoint targets as often, or use quick hands, or switch to space to open up the ground. They tend to win the ball in their area and blindly kick long.

In the eighties, there was a revolution in the speed of ball movement, and the game became fast, furious, skillful and tough. Yet it was still rooted in a century-old tradition that the most important thing each week was to go out and beat your man. As both Schwab and Flanigan point out, coaches hadn't yet devised the means to clog up the game.

Defence meant tackling hard. Team defence meant tackling so hard that your tackles added up to 40. It's not that watching modern footy is terrible. The skills that modern players can execute under previously inconceivable levels of pressure defy belief, and low scores often mean close and exciting games. It's just that for those of us who saw what footy was—space to move, the thrill of the contest, smaller packs, higher marks—the balance is wrong. There are too many bodies, too much heat at the source, and not enough Langford versus Ablett, standing under a high ball, just the two of them, a premiership hinging on the outcome.

Even the day after the 1989 Grand Final, Rohan Connolly in *The Age* gave a sense that this game was a beautiful anachronism, that the coaches were coming, and this was the end of an era. He wrote:

"Let's also be thankful for the simplicity with which the match was played. We have come to expect Grand Finals to resemble games of chess, but Allan Jeans and Malcolm Blight had enough faith in their players to leave most pieces on the board untouched. What a difference to the elimination final between Melbourne and Collingwood, when John Northey and Leigh Matthews spent half a game attempting to cover their deficiencies with elaborate games of cat and mouse and ended up only confusing their players and themselves. On Saturday, moves were made only when absolutely necessary."

A few years ago, I was MC at a mid-season event at Hawthorn that featured the master coach of the club's present golden era, Alastair Clarkson. He was asked a question from the floor about the look of the modern game, the congestion, and his role in contributing to it. Clarkson is the architect of what's now known as 'Clarko's Cluster', a pioneering, most-of-ground, zone defence credited with winning his team the 2008 flag.

Clarkson's reply to the interlocutor stayed with me. He said it wasn't like he didn't love watching games like the 1989 Grand Final. As a footy fan, he loved one-on-one contests, forwards kicking big bags of goals, blokes going head-to-head all over the ground, Ablett jumping on his opponent's head. But to his mind, as a coach, the surprising thing wasn't that there were now complex defensive structures in footy. The surprising thing to Clarkson was that for 100 years we'd let them go one-on-one. Why did Peter Hudson stand next to one bloke in the square, just him and the full-back, when he was twice as good a footballer, and he'd kick 10 goals? Why did the coaches just let that happen? The job, Clarkson said, was to win! Why didn't they just stick a heap of other blokes in Hudson's way? For him, that was the miracle. What's happened recently is merely the inevitable evolution of the game.

That rang true to me. Coaches are in the business of winning, and now there are so, so many coaches and assistants, and so, so many hours in which to coach. Which is why watching the 1989 Grand Final is doubly nostalgic. Not only is it the game at its most beautiful, it is a beauty that will never be seen again.

61

JUST ONE SATURDAY IN SEPTEMBER

If Geelong was unlucky to strike one of the greatest teams of all time on 30 September 1989, it didn't get much luckier over the next few years. This team of such promise would make three more Grand Finals in the next six years and lose all of them. One of the greatest collections of footballing talent in that or any other decade was destined to be remembered as a team that specialised in losing, rather than celebrated as a team that specialised in pure sporting entertainment.

By 1991, the West Coast Eagles are the best team in the country. They win three more games over the home and away season that year than both Hawthorn and Geelong. And yet the Eagles fumble their chance in the Grand Final, the "too old, too slow" Hawks exploiting their opponents' inexperience to rise for one final hurrah. Geelong lose to Hawthorn in that Finals Series, by two points, and then by 15 to the Eagles. In *Comeback*, James Button ponders whether, for Geelong, this is the one that got away.

By the next season the Mick Malthouse-coached Eagles are a team on a mission, stung by the defeat of '91. They're massively talented, almost a *de facto* State of Origin team, and they're also just massive. The Eagles players come back from their Grand Final defeat visibly bigger—beefed up, the subject of suspicious whispers; they are not to be intimidated again. Blight's Cats finish on top after the home and away season, win two finals, but lose the Grand Final to the Eagles by 28 points. Blight is so disappointed he fails to front in the rooms afterwards.

In 1993 Blight obsesses over defence. He's moody and angry. He departs from the game plan that made Geelong an attacking phenomenon and the team performs poorly. It's not until an angry and honest player meeting after a 71-point loss to St Kilda in round 16 at Waverley that Blight apologises and takes responsibility for a poor season. "I've cost you the year," he tells his senior players. The story is retold vividly and quite brilliantly in the Malcolm Blight episode of the podcast, *1993: The Greatest Season That Was*. The team resets to its old game plan and storms home to win its last five games. But the Cats, arguably the best team in the competition by that point, miss the finals on percentage. Kevin Sheedy's Baby Bombers sneak under everyone's guard and pinch the flag. It would have been a good year to be in the finals.

In 1994 it's another Grand Final for Blight's Cats, facing off against the Eagles again. West Coast has finished top, three games ahead of Geelong. The points for and points against comparison over the home and away season is interesting. Geelong is the attacking force, scoring 325 points more than West Coast. But on the defensive side, the Eagles are superior by a whopping 532 points. As Blight concedes, defence was always the problem for the Cats, how many goals they conceded. Think of those great West Coast backs—Glenn Jakovich, Guy McKenna, John Worsfold and Ashley McIntosh. In the Grand Final McIntosh keeps Ablett to one goal from five kicks and

West Coast win the game by 80 points. After 145 games Blight, the wonder coach, is finished at Geelong.

"You think geez, it was a wonderful era, we played some sparkling footy, some great players," says Blight. "I think people really enjoyed the footy and it was winning ... We won 61 per cent of our games. It's a pretty good strike rate ... just one Saturday in September ... just one. Yeah, would I? Yeah course I would have ... I would have preferred to have got one."

62

IDIOSYNCRASIES

In 1995, under Blight's successor, Gary Ayres, Geelong is still thereabouts. In the home and away season the Cats are again only the second-best team. Unfortunately, there's a new Emperor, and it's Carlton, which wins an incredible 20 games from 22—four more than Geelong. That's measurable superiority, and so it proves on Grand Final day. The Cats lose by 10 goals. Again, this group of players has pushed up against one of history's great teams.

It's Ablett's last great year. He kicks 122 goals in 22 games at an average of five and a half a game. He's 34 years of age. Ayres, the man who almost knocked him out in the first ten minutes of the 1989 Grand Final, and whose father coached Ablett in the Drouin Under-12s, now has the job of harnessing Ablett's talent.

"We are only one-year difference in age," says Ayres. Then he grins. "It was interesting, I guess." Ayres recalls one home game at Geelong where Ablett was ticked off by the team manager as being present, but then as game time approached, he had suddenly disappeared. "Phil Walsh, the late Phil Walsh was our strength and conditioning coach," says Ayres, "and he wanted to warm the players up, and he's come to me with a bit of a worried look on his face and said, 'I can't find Gazza anywhere'."

"'I've looked everywhere,' Walsh told the coach. "I've looked in the toilets, I've looked in the medical room, I've looked in the physio room, he's not in the plunge pool, he's not anywhere."

Ayres joined the search. Finally, he tried a small boot-studder's room, down a little hallway, the last door on the left before the players' changeroom. "The door was closed and I've opened it," says Ayres, "And here's Gazza, with a full pie with sauce, sitting on the bench, and another half-eaten one, and I've said, 'Gazza, come on, we've got go do the warm-up,' and he's said, 'Yeah, all right'. And he's chowing down on this pie, and he comes out and kicks six goals."

He's the most compelling player of all time, Ablett. So spectacular, so gifted, so enigmatic, and yet so difficult. Ayres was merely the next, and last, mortal coach who was expected to manoeuvre around him. Ablett made watching footy so much fun, the most fun, and yet his team's lack of premiership success in his time raises a recurring question. Did the accommodation of his eccentricities and whims hurt the team? Did the interests of an individual compromise the interests of the group? Was Ablett a factor in Geelong failing to take the final giant step?

Of course, you can look at it the other way too. Ablett was granted allowances by his coaches, nursed through his periods of indifference and distraction, and he repaid the Cats with a thousand goals and four Grand Finals—unfurling, in one of them, the greatest goal spree of all. Who knows, without the Great Gazza, the Cats might have been anchored mid-table.

I like Couch's comment on *Open Mike*: "A lot of blokes couldn't cop him...because he was different, the way he wouldn't handball and wouldn't train, the way he was different and got away with things. But for me, I was happy for him to play because I played in a lot of Grand Finals. I was lucky to play with him."

Ablett retired at the end of 1996. Almost the same week, Blight was announced as coach of Adelaide Crows. On the day Blight was appointed, Couch rang his close friend Mark Bairstow. He recalled the conversation on *Open Mike*: "They'll win it, these blokes. They've got the side for it. All they need is one bloke to go and do it, and that's Blighty."

So, it proved. The Crows went back-to-back in their new coach's first two seasons—the first team to do it since the 1989 Hawks.

63

THE SECRET LAIR

Allan Jeans died on 13 July 2011, which was a Wednesday. Earlier that week, Robert DiPierdomenico had been out to the Lynbrook Park Convalescent Home in Cranbourne to visit him, along with '89 premiership cohorts Jason Dunstall and Peter Curran. Dipper says Jeans was in good spirits and that three stars of Hawthorn's great era to come were there too: Lance Franklin, Jarryd Roughead and Grant Birchall.

Jeans teased Dipper, which was one of his favourite activities: "The press, they always wanted to know why I took Dipper off at three-quarter time, and I'd have to say, 'No, he was still out there'." They had a fresh audience, and Dipper and Jeans held court.

They shared the trusty 'lace-up jumper story', the one about Dipper being offered $15,000 in the mid-eighties by a manufacturer of old-fashioned lace-up jumpers to wear a prototype in a big game. It was big money in those days, and Dipper said yes but thought he should clear it with the coach first. He knocked on the door of the coach's room. Jeans was in a match committee meeting with Brian Coleman and reserves coach Des Meagher. Dipper cleared his throat: "Umm, Jeansy, I just want to let you know that I'm gonna wear a lace-up jumper this week—I got a bit of a deal—I just thought I should let you know." A silence fell over the room as Jeans pondered the news. "What felt like an eternity, it was probably ten seconds," says Dipper. When Jeans responded he did so quietly: "Mmmmm, you better not ask me, son, you better ask Des Meagher." DiPierdomenico was momentarily stumped. "I'm thinking, 'Why do I fucking ask Des Meagher, he's the reserves coach?'" Finally, the penny dropped. Dipper never wore the jumper. "That man," Dipper said to the young Hawks while pointing at Jeans. "That old bastard over there cost me fifteen grand!"

They hammed it up. Jeans said to the room that Dipper was never one of his favourites, so Dipper squeezed the tubes that were coming out of his nose. "If I die now," Jeans said, pretending to gasp, "I'll be the happiest person in the world."

Dipper was in Brisbane when he got the call from his wife, Cheryl. Jeans had passed away. "I just felt really lonely," says Dipper. "He was a marvellous person, a marvellous person. He threw up challenges, and he taught me to live the Hawthorn way."

Brereton's last visit to Lynbrook is similarly burned into his memory. "I remember he put his arm around me and put his forehead on my shoulder, and he said, 'I just want to thank you for what you did, it means the world to me.'

Brereton gets emotional talking about these last moments with his coach. He says: "I thanked him back. I'm the one who should be thanking him."

There's that reciprocal love and respect, a bond forged over 35 years. I think of the red Ferrari and the peroxide blond perm, and the years in the nightclubs, and ask Dermott how a man as humble and austere as Jeans coped with a young man of such exuberance and flamboyance. Brereton laughs. "Here's a little-known truth about Allan Jeans," he says. "And I learnt it once when we were playing indoor cricket with a tennis ball and a bat. He was a left-handed batsman, and somebody bowled to him, and he went down on one knee to hit a cover drive with a tennis ball. And the next ball, he went onto the back foot and he waved a beautifully stylish bat. Now, knowing my cricket, he was a show-pony batsman! So, everything about Jeansy's mantra of team—keep it dour, keep it simple—he actually had a touch of lair in himself. So, he liked the lairs, but he wanted to harness them. Think of his five favourites. He had Dipper and me in there!"

Ayres remembers his last conversation, too. "I had a phone call with him … just to make sure everything was okay to go out and see him, and the doctors said, 'No, he's not having any visitors, only family.' We chatted for 15 minutes, and it got really tough because he knew and I knew that I would never speak to him again, and more than likely not see him again, and it got to the point where the words … and I remember them as clear as yesterday, I said, 'For everything I've ever achieved in footy, coaching and playing, I just owe it all to you'. And his comments back to me were, 'No, I owe everything to you.' And that's the mark of Allan Jeans. I got off the phone after I said goodbye to him, and I started crying, because I knew it was the last time."

As Brereton and Ayres become emotional, I think not only of their bond with Jeans, but those forged by hundreds of players across four decades of League coaching—how many other lives he touched like this. Brian Coleman says that whenever he went to visit Jeans at Lynbrook, there were just as many St Kilda players present as there were from Hawthorn. Says Coleman: "Whatever club he was at, he was loved."

"I loved him," says Platten. "He became a father figure to all of us. Both on and off the ground. If you had a problem, you could always go to him. Some coaches… it's hard for players to go up and confront the coach and tell him what you're thinking … He was way before his time. He was amazing."

John Kennedy Jnr said his goodbye, too. "It was a couple of weeks before he died. He thanked me for what I had done for him as a player and said that he wanted me to do the eulogy." Kennedy thinks he was chosen because he was President of the Hawthorn Past Players Association. "He was calculated again, I think. He could have asked anyone to do it—Leigh Matthews, Jason, Dermott, Johnny Platten—but because I had a role within the football club that was impartial, he asked me to do it."

The funeral was held in the Members' dining room at the MCG, a week after Jeans died. The great orator was sent off with some stirring eulogies, and a rousing rendition of Schubert's *Ave Maria*, sung by a soloist from the Victorian Police Choir. The coffin did a lap of the ground before it departed. Kennedy was funny and anecdotal, and finished with some lovely words, as he choked back tears:

> "The lessons he taught us to be successful on and off the field have been used by each and every one of us at various times since we left behind those halcyon days at Hawthorn.
>
> The benefits of persistence, a sense of responsibility, commitment to family, how to win with humility, how to lose with dignity, without excuses. How to manage people and how to lead, to name just a few...
>
> It's difficult to put into words the varying degrees of influence that Yab had on our lives. But in reflecting over the years it would be fair to say that for most of my teammates and I, he, outside of our parents, had the biggest influence on the way we operate today.
>
> Men such as Allan Jeans are a rarity and we will be forever grateful that we were in the right place at the right time to enjoy one of the greatest characters that we will ever meet. He leaves us all with wonderful memories and achievements.
>
> On behalf of all us scallywags, Yab, our sincerest thanks and goodbye, our leader and friend."[3]

---

3   Find John Kennedy's complete obituary via Speakola *https://bit.ly/2sSS4Jg*

POSTSCRIPT

There's a familiar anecdote from Hawthorn's 1989 Grand Final victory, a story that has been told and retold down the decades, perhaps more often than any other off-field footy story. So well-worn is this tale that's it almost like 'The Aristocrats' joke. For Hawthorn people, there's no novelty in the punchline, you only listen for the twists and turns the teller might take in getting you there.

Anyway, I'm going to lay it down once and for all, just because this is a book, and if I've learned anything from the monks who wrote *The Book of Kells*, it's that stories on paper last longer than stories told at 1am to drunk people at premiership reunions. So here it is, the most oft told end-of-season trip story in the history of end-of-season trips.

It starts off with an exhibition match loss at Joe Robbie Stadium in Miami in October, two weeks after the Grand Final. The Bombers beat Hawthorn by 14 points. Still, nobody really cares—not the thousands of people who aren't sitting in the empty banks of orange bleachers, and certainly not Hawthorn's premiership stars who are, as you might imagine, still pretty bloody happy.

Allan Jeans is happy too and sends his players out to have a good night. "It's been a great year," he says. "Enjoy yourselves tonight. But whatever you do, don't get yourselves in trouble, and if you find yourselves in any sort of trouble, make sure you call me."

Over the course of the evening, a group of players decide to scale the fence of another hotel in order to cool off in the pool. Hotel security is alerted and the players are booted out. They hail a taxi to return to the team hotel, sodden in every sense of the word.

The taxi contains: Anthony Condon, a tough young midfielder who's had a breakout season and an excellent Grand Final; Sean Ralphsmith, a Haileybury College product who is an honest footballer, but has played just one Senior game, and that was at the end of 1988; Ray Jencke, a 53-gamer but, on Grand Final day, not picked in Hawthorn's best 20; and Jason Dunstall, star full-forward, who's coming off 138 goals for the year—more than any player in a generation.

The quartet arrives in the vicinity of the hotel, and whether they've lost their wallets during the swimming adventure or are merely exercising a lack of judgment after umpteen standard drinks, they make a poor decision: they decide to ditch the taxi without paying.

They open the doors and start running. Condon, who is, according to at least one teammate, "a bit more street-smart than the others" peels off by himself. He'll eventually take a winding route back to the hotel and avoid any further misadventures. His three cohorts don't. They bolt straight for the hotel—yes, the same hotel whose name they slurred to the taxi driver when they entered the cab.

Up in his room, Jeans is woken by the hotel phone. "Sir, we've got a member of the Florida Police Force down here asking for you." Jeans throws on a hotel gown and hurries down to the lobby. There's a commotion. In the forecourt there are multiple squad cars, lights swirling, and in the headlights of one of the cars, a line-up of bedraggled footballers, hands raised: two young rookies flank Jeans's undisputed star goalkicker, coming off back-to-back Coleman Medal years.

"Stay exactly where you are!" an agitated policeman is shouting. Miami is the drug crime capital of America. When the cops make an arrest, they don't muck around.

Jeans enters the fray, explaining his ex-cop credentials to the sergeant in charge, and tells him about the premiership celebrations, that his boys are just here on a footy trip, and asks the cop to exercise restraint.

The sergeant isn't happy. He says, "If any of these three boys try and run, we'll shoot 'em!"

Jeans's reply comes without hesitation: "Whatever you do, don't shoot the fat bloke in the middle."

And that's the end of the story.

ACKNOWLEDGEMENTS

Many thanks to the Hawthorn and Geelong players, coaches and officials who assisted me with this project.

These include my interviewees: Dean Anderson, Gary Ayres, Dermott Brereton, Andy Collins, Peter Curran, Robert DiPierdomenico, Damian Drum, Terry Gay, John Kennedy Jnr, Chris Langford, Greg Madigan, Scott Maginness, John Platten, Peter Schwab, Paul Cooper, Malcolm Blight, Tim Darcy, Bruce Lindner, Darren Flanigan, Brian Coleman, Chris Wittman, Mark Yeates, John Origlasso, Caroline Wilson, Steve Perkin, Shane Templeton and David Parkin.

Thanks to Bob Gartland for sourcing contact numbers for Geelong players and to John Kennedy Jnr and Andy Gowers for doing the same for the Hawks.

Thank you to Peter Dickson, director of *The Final Story* documentary, who not only made a brilliant film about the game but shared all his interview transcripts with me.

I'm grateful to the authors of all source material listed in the

ACKNOWLEDGEMENTS

bibliography, but particular thanks go to James Button, John Harms of *The Footy Almanac* and Brett Meyers of *The Mongrel Punt* who lent effort and advice.

Thank you to my editor, Russell Jackson. Your enthusiasm, knowledge, encouragement and talent got me to the line. It's a lucky author who gets to be edited by one of the country's finest sportswriters.

Thanks to the publisher at The Slattery Media Group, Geoff Slattery for inviting me to the project. Your contribution to sport and literature has been immense.

To my dad, Ray Wilson, you have my love and appreciation for all the encouragement and support over so many years, including taking on first reader duties with this one.

Thank you to my wife, Tamsin, and to our four kids Polly, Harry, Jack and Alice—you all rallied to help me navigate a tight deadline.

And thanks to all the players who played—what a game. It makes me so happy.

There will be an audio documentary version of the interviews that comprise this book, released as a podcast called '1989, The Great Grand Final'. Stay tuned.

Tony Wilson's other sports books and sports novels, *Players*, *Making News*, and *Australia United; Adventures at World Cup Germany 2006*, are available through *iTunes* and *Amazon* and *Kobo* (eBook format) or through Tony's website (tonywilson.com.au).

His footy books for kids are *A Boy Called Bob* (with Bob Murphy) and *The Selwood Boys*.

Tony also co-directed the footy history feature documentary, 'The Galahs' about the 1967 tour of Ireland by VFL footballers. Distributed through Madman Entertainment.

THE 1989 FINALS OF HAWTHORN AND GEELONG

GEELONG

Qualifying Final (September 10), MCG

Geelong	2.4 6.5 7.7 11.15 **(81)**
Essendon	5.5 12.9 19.12 24.13 **(157)**

Goals: Ablett 3, Hamilton 3, Exell, Brownless, Burns, G.Hocking, Bews.
Best: Lindner, Bews, Ablett, Bos.
(Crowd: 75,861)

First Semi-Final (September 17), MCG

Geelong	3.3 8.8 12.11 22.21 **(153)**
Melbourne	1.5 3.11 8.16 12.18 **(90)**

Goals: Ablett 7, Stoneham 4, Cameron 3, Brownless 3, Hamilton 2, Darcy, Bews, Couch.
Best: Hamilton, Bews, Stoneham, Ablett.
(Crowd: 69,082)

Preliminary Final (September 23), Waverley Park

Geelong	6.4 13.12 19.15 24.20 **(164)**
Essendon	4.3 6.4 6.9 10.10 **(70)**

Goals: Ablett 8, Brownless 4, Stoneham 3, Scott 2, Couch 2, G.Hocking 2, Cameron, Bairstow, Bews.
Best: Ablett, G.Hocking, Stoneham, Bairstow, Bews, Bruns, Lindner.
(Crowd: 67,892)

HAWTHORN

Second Semi-Final (September 16), Waverley Park

Hawthorn	3.2 8.4 13.10 16.16 **(112)**
Essendon	5.4 7.6 9.6 11.10 **(76)**

Goals: Dunstall 6, Buckenara 3, Curran 2, Pritchard 2, Anderson, G.Dear, DiPierdomenico.
Best: Platten, Anderson, Ayres, Buckenara, Dear, Pritchard, Dunstall.
(Crowd: 66,003)

The Grand Final (September 30), MCG

Hawthorn	8.4 12.9 18.13 21.18 **(144)**
Geelong	2.0 7.2 13.7 21.12 **(138)**

Goals:
Hawthorn: Dunstall 4, Anderson 4, Buckenara 4, Brereton 3, Curran 3, DiPierdomenico, Wittman, Morrissey.
Geelong: Ablett 9, Brownless 2, Stoneham 2, Hamilton 2, Cameron 2, Bews, Bairstow, Bruns, Flanigan.
(Crowd: 94,796)
Best:
Hawthorn: Pritchard, Anderson, DiPierdomenico, Buckenara, Dunstall, Curran.
Geelong: Ablett, Lindner, Flanigan, Hamilton, Bews, Couch.
Coaches: Allan Jeans (Hawthorn), Malcolm Blight (Geelong).
Umpires: Peter Carey, Bryan Sheehan.
Norm Smith Medal: Gary Ablett.

ACKNOWLEDGEMENTS

1989 GRAND FINAL GAME STATS

HAWTHORN

PLAYER	KICKS	MARKS	HANDBALLS	DISPOSALS	GOALS	TACKLES
Dean Anderson	13	3	2	15	4	1
Gary Ayres	9	1	0	9	0	2
Dermott Brereton	9	4	0	9	3	2
Gary Buckenara	13	4	7	20	4	3
Andy Collins	7	1	0	7	0	2
Anthony Condon	8	6	8	16	0	3
Peter Curran	10	3	5	15	3	3
Greg Dear	6	2	4	10	0	1
Robert DiPierdomenico	13	5	5	18	1	5
Jason Dunstall	8	8	1	9	4	2
John Kennedy	5	4	5	10	0	3
Chris Langford	9	6	4	13	0	0
Greg Madigan	2	0	2	4	0	0
Scott Maginness	5	2	2	7	0	2
Chris Mew	10	3	2	12	0	2
James Morrissey	7	2	6	13	1	2
John Platten	3	0	1	4	0	2
Darrin Pritchard	20	4	0	20	0	4
Michael Tuck	8	2	3	11	0	6
Chris Wittman	10	1	3	13	1	2
Totals	**175**	**61**	**60**	**235**	**21**	**47**

GEELONG

Gary Ablett	12	8	3	15	9	3
Mark Bairstow	12	2	3	15	1	2
Andrew Bews	19	3	8	27	1	2
Mark Bos	9	1	1	10	0	1
Damian Bourke	1	1	0	1	0	0
Billy Brownless	4	3	0	4	2	0
Neville Bruns	12	3	2	14	1	3
David Cameron	8	2	3	11	2	1
Paul Couch	13	2	9	22	0	0
Tim Darcy	2	0	1	3	0	1
Darren Flanigan	13	9	2	15	1	0
Shane Hamilton	16	2	2	18	2	3
Garry Hocking	6	1	7	13	0	1
Steve Hocking	2	2	7	9	0	3
Bruce Lindner	18	5	7	25	0	1
Spiro Malakellis	9	3	6	15	0	0
Michael Schulze	2	1	0	2	0	1
Robert Scott	5	2	3	8	0	2
Barry Stoneham	8	5	4	12	2	0
Mark Yeates	5	2	7	12	0	1
Totals	**176**	**57**	**75**	**251**	**21**	**25**

• Game scores and best players courtesy of the AFL Record Guide to Season 2019 (Ed. Michael Lovett, published by Crocmedia) • Match Statistics sourced from *afltables.com*

1989 GRAND FINAL LINE-UP

HAW	B:	A.Collins	C.Langford	G.Ayres
GEEL	F:	D.Cameron	B.Brownless	R.Scott
HAW	HB:	S.Maginness	C.Mew	J.Kennedy
GEEL	HF:	G.Hocking	B.Stoneham	G.Ablett
HAW	C:	D.Pritchard	A.Condon	R.DiPierdomenico
GEEL	C:	N.Bruns	P.Couch	M.Yeates
HAW	HF:	D.Anderson	D.Brereton	G.Buckenara
GEEL	HB:	M.Bos	M.Schulze	B.Lindner
HAW	F:	P.Curran	J.Dunstall	C.Wittman
GEEL	B:	S.Malakellis	T.Darcy	S.Hocking
HAW	R:	G.Dear	M.Tuck (capt)	J.Platten
GEEL	R:	D.Bourke (capt)	M.Bairstow	A.Bews

HAW **IC:** J.Morrissey, G.Madigan **Coach:** Allan Jeans

GEEL **IC:** D.Flanigan, S.Hamilton **Coach:** Malcolm Blight

BIBLIOGRAPHY

BOOKS

James Button, Comeback: *The Fall and Rise of Geelong*, MUP, 2016

John Harms, *Loose Men Everywhere*, Text Publishing, 2002

Harry and Michael Gordon, *One for All: The Story of the Hawthorn Football Club*, Wilkinson Publishing, 2009

Tim Watson and James Weston, *Malcolm Blight: Player, Coach, Legend*, Hardie Grant, 2011

Garry Linnell, *Playing God, the rise and fall of Gary Ablett*, Harper Collins, 2004

Steve Lawrence, *Make Your Mark—five hidden keys to great leadership* (Wilkinson Publishing, 2019)

ARTICLES

HB Meyers, *An Oral History of the Geelong v Hawthorn Rivalry Part Two -1989*, themongrelpunt.com

Jonathan Horn, *1989 and all that: Remembering the Greatest Grand Final*, The Guardian, 23 September 2014

Geoff Slattery, *Jeans New Coach of Hawks*, The Age 1 October, 1980

Gary Linnell, *Why Geelong Lets Ablett Play football His Way*, The Age, 7 June 1986

Garry Linnell, *Street-wise kid prepares for life after football*, Times on Sunday, 12 July 1987

Garry Linnell, *Outgunned And Out Flanked, The Hawks Out-Thought, Too*, The Age, 27 September 1987

Martin Flanagan, *There We Were, Like Witnesses At A Hanging*, The Age, 26 September 1988

Martin Flanagan, *Hawks Win Purges '87 – A Triumph For Commitment*, The Herald, 26 September 1988,

Caroline Wilson and Gerard Wright, *Blight Wins Without Fuss And Fury*, The Age, 13 July 1989

Martin Flanagan, *Ablett: As Different As A Sunny, Warm Day In The Midst Of Winter*, The Age, 25 September 1989

Rohan Connolly, *A Sporting Contest That Had The Lot*, The Age, 2 October 1989

Caroline Wilson, *Ablett: From Exile To Centre Stage*, The Sunday Age, 1 October 1989

Mark Robinson, *Dermott Brereton on heartbreak and his violent father's cocaine abuse*, Herald Sun, 22 May 2010.

FILMS/TV

Stephen Phillips, *Inside the Battle of 89 1989 VFL Grand Final Reunion Special*, Australian Football Video, 1999

Peter Dickson, *The Final Story 1989*, AFL Media, 2013

Mike Sheahan, *Open Mike*, with Paul Couch, 15 September 2014

Mike Sheahan, *Open Mike*, with Dermott Brereton, 2012

STATISTICS

afltables.com, australianfootball.com